T0163890

New Visions of Priesting

An Interview with Bob Wilkinson

New Visions of Priesting

An Interview with Bob Wilkinson

Adelaide
2022

Text copyright ©2022 remains jointly with ATF Press and PR Wilkinson. All rights reserved. Except for any fair dealing under the Copyright Act, no part of the publication may be reproduced by any means without prior permission. Inquiries should be made in the first instance with the publisher.

Photographs copyright: PR Wilkinson.
Cover Design: Ross Row and Gabriel Bueno Siqueira

Cardijn Studies: On the Church in the World of Today
Volume 3, 2022

The Cardijn Studies journal is a refereed journal which aims to document the history of the Jocist, Cardijn inspired, lay movements both historically and in the present day as well as the examining the rich tradition of Catholic Social teaching on the Church in the world of today. Articles cover a range of areas: the spirituality, methodology and the history of these traditions and movements in the Church and in society.

Editorial Board

Editor: Hilary Dominic Regan

- **Assistant Professor Kevin Ahern**, Manhattan College, New York, USA.
- **Dr Ana Maria Bidegain**, Professor of Latin American Religions at Florida International University, USA.
- **Fr Michael Deeb OP**, South Africa
- **David Moloney**, professional historian, Cardijn Community Australia executive member
- **Stefan Gigacz**, Secretary Cardijn Community, Australia

Business Manager, Editor and Publisher:
Mr Hilary Dominic Regan, ATF Press Publishing Group, PO Box 234, Brompton, SA 5007, Australia.
Email: hdregan@atf.org.au

ISBN: 978-1-922737-33-5 Soft
          978-1-922737-34-2 Hard
          978-1-922737-35-9 Epub
          978-1-922737-36-6 Pdf

Published and edited by

www.atfpress.com

Making a lasting impact
An imprint of the ATF Press Publishing Group
owned by ATF (Australia) Ltd.
PO Box 234
Brompton, SA 5007
Australia
ABN 90 116 359 963

Contents

Editorial

This edition of the *Cardijn Studies* journal is quite unique. In the years since the last edition there has been a change of editor. I would like to thank and acknowledge the work done by Stefan Gigacz as editor.

This edition of the journal is a series of interviews with Bob Wilkinson. Bob, an Adelaide born Catholic priest, is a long-time follower of Joseph Cardijn and chaplain for close on seventy years of lay movements inspired by the founder of the Young Christian Worker movement, Belgium Catholic priest Joseph Cardijn and the Jocist tradition. Bob has been chaplain at various times to workers in the Young Christian Workers (YCW) movement, students in the secondary Young Christian Students (YCS) movement, students in the tertiary based Tertiary Young Christian Students (TCYS) movement, and also adults and family in Adelaide based Christian Life Movement (CLM). During this long period of involvement, accompanying lay people in the Catholic Church, he was also a university chaplain, chaplain to the Tertiary Catholic Federation of Australia (TCFA) and chaplain of the Teams. In all of these involvements he had, at times, local, national and international responsibilities. Later he would be involved in various initiatives in Catholic Church parish renewal in the Adelaide diocese, inspired by principles of the Jocist tradition, in the Basic Christian Communities (BECs) and Neighbourhood Church. All of these you will find mentioned in the interviews in this volume of Cardijn Studies.

Over his lifetime a constant in his life has been accompanying lay people in movements of formation and renewal in the Church, ones with a global focus on the mission of humanity in the world. All of this coming from his early reading of the works of Joseph Cardijn. From Cardijn it has been a focus on a 'lay, lay, Church', of 'the lay people in the Church and the Church in the lay people'.

Bob has been heavily influenced by his wide reading, since seminary days, of French theological and sociological literature and of groups in the Catholic Church who have been run by lay people, for lay people with lay people. Reading this literature while studying in the seminary, he saw the Catholic Church and his ministry, within this lens. His commitment to the lay movements stayed with him from seminary days right up till now. In a few months time, after this edition of the journal is released, Bob will be ninety years of age.

This series of interviews made as a book is chronological in nature starting with his early life right through to his time with the Neighbourhood Church prior to his semi-retirement, and outlines Bob's vision of being a priest, looking at new ways of 'priesting' in changing environments from when he was first ordained in the 1950s. All this done while totally faithful to the Catholic tradition, of it being universal in nature and, at the same time, totally devoted throughout this life to what it means to accompany, not direct, laypeople in work, home and leisure. This especially so in a post Vatican II era.

Bob was heavily involved in the organisation of the 1958 visit of Joseph Cardijn to Adelaide. His writing of the booklet accompanying this visit, led to his being suggested by Fr PP Kelly to be the replacement editor of *The Southern Cross* newspaper in the Adelaide diocese. He held this position for many years while also being chaplain at Cabra College and involved with a vigorous secondary school YCS there.

Given Bob's faithful reading and following of Joseph Cardijn and the Jocist tradition, it is entirely appropriate these interviews are being written up in the *Cardijn Studies* journal. The journal, in sync with the ideas Bob outlines in these interviews, has a subtitle of *On the Church in the World of Today*.

These interviews have taken some time to get to where they are now in print. Over five years ago, ATF Press began a series of one-on-one interviews with Bob, sitting down with him and taking copious notes. This was time consuming and for a variety of reasons was left to one side after eight months of roughly monthly meetings.

With the advent of 'zoom', twelve hourly zoom sessions were conducted over a number of months from early on in the COVID pandemic, in 2020. ATF Press devised the questions and Bob responded to them. It was decided a chronological approach to his life would be pursued. At that time ATF Press did not have the facility to do a quick automatic transcript. So for each hour of a zoom session it meant roughly two to three hours were spent listening to and typing up the session. It was a conversational style of interview which did not translate well to a written text.

After some many hours of editing the Zoom session recording, there was a process of in-house proof reading which also took some time. A hiatus occurred and then over a period of six to eight months Bob began revising the text that was given to him by ATF Press. This involved Bob reading the text and the ATF Press making the corrections, additions etc on a lap top computer while Bob spoke. It was time consuming.

Many revisions occurred over time, things taken out, others included, and the interviews rearranged. The chronological structure remained constant, an editorial decision made by ATF Press. Later an introduction and then a conclusion were added. At the same time, hours were spent on a cover design later to be replaced by the one that is now the present cover. During this time, long-time friend and colleague from CLM days, through to the BEC's and the Neighbourhood Church, Sr Ruth Egar RSM, and past student at Cabra College, who had been in YCS groups there, Patricia Cramp, along with others, were proof reading different parts of the text. ATF Press acknowledges all who had a part in this project. Thank you all for your commitment and the many hours that were put in over a considerable amount of time, at times looking at a manuscript, or part there-of, more than once.

At one stage it was thought this volume would come out before the second session of the Plenary Council of the Catholic Church in Australia in 2022, but the editing process meant the publication date had to be moved. In many ways the themes and issues of Bob's vision of being a priest, of 'priesting', are there for any time to be read by all those in the Catholic Church and wider.

As Editor and Publisher of the journal, I take full responsibility for any mistakes within these interviews. I thank Bob for making his time available to ATF Press over the past five years, for the time he has spent checking texts, re-writing and making the manuscript more accessible. The final responsibility for the manuscript remains with the Editor and Publisher.

Hilary Dominic Regan
Editor and Publisher
30 August 2022

Bob Wilkinson with Joseph Cardijn in Adelaide, 1958

1

The Story of These Stories

ATF Press: By way of an introduction to this book, let us look at some of the key issues that have influenced you over the years which are spoken about at length in the interviews.

PR Wilkinson: This book has become the story of my shift in thinking over a lifetime from 'Christians living their life in the world' to 'Christians humbly taking their special part in the great global mission of humanity'.

In the language of theology, we grow as Christians by understanding and humbly embracing our part in the mission of humanity. It was not only believers or the Church that raised the banners for our planet. The saints of today are those who have raised the alarm to save creation, so many of whom are of no Christian persuasion.

To speak of the 'mission of humanity' may sound novel, even vaguely making less of the Church's mission. But the first instruction to Adam and Eve is not a list of what not to do. It is tasks to achieve for God, the original human mission. This mission is twofold as it remains, a twofold mission to nature and to one another, to themselves and to nature, 'Be fruitful and multiply: and fill the earth and subdue it'. This primal mission is never revoked, but subsumed in further missions of God to humanity

Pope Francis' encyclical *Be Praised* is for any open-minded person, compelling evidence that Christians are indeed in the forefront of the movement to care for our common home. But the Pope can go down in history particularly as the leading voice for this—that care for our common global home is inextricable from global equality.

Francis weaves a beautiful argument of how closely knit are the human and environmental threads. In EF Schumacher's formula, the desperate need of earth's beauty, fruitfulness and survival to be saved is widely recognised. Less urgently appreciated is how these and the spiritual unity of humanity intertwine.

We are not just another species. In the ancient Bible story, the arrival of humanity has its own day, a little less than the angels, a little more than the beasts. Scientists recognise our uniqueness. This whole epoch of the planet is called the Anthropocene, the Human-marked. Not that science can claim to have discovered this. Australia's own First Nation has forever sung its ancient song-lines of our mob and its origins intimately connected to our land.

Where does this leave the Gospel of Christ? Polls show a large proportion of our population assume our ancient faith is only hanging on desperately.

However, in those polls, significant numbers of Catholics are unswerving from the tradition following Pope Francis, that there is, *within any authentic global ecology, an irreplaceable religious vitality.*

This does not mean some private space for believers. To a degree we have never depthed before, to be faithful to Jesus Christ means whole-hearted planetary ecology, where the defence of plants and animals and climate is crowned by global commitment to human equality and dignity. We need to save the human species, as much as any species. But we are not just another animal species. We need one another. All animals do. But we need one another as more than animals. We are the species made to understand love and to value beauty and to choose the planet in ways unique to us. We have responsibility. Other animals do not.

Creation is more than the Big Bang. It is the endless process of energy and direction that a name like 'evolution' could too easily reduce down to some materialist orthodoxy. *Pace* Hamlet, there are more things in heaven and earth than are dreamt of in our philosophy, our science and our theology.

This series of interviews is an account of how one undistinguished priest's tracks seemed to him to have been crisscrossing an unfolding future, a future calling our universal Church to new universality. If as Church we can humbly answer our call to be fellow pilgrims of humanity our identity will be more than defended.

The Catholic Church has often wandered disastrously from its call, sometimes crucified, sometimes crucifying. But century after century, by the power of Christ crucified and risen, our Church reappears on the pilgrim way. God is forever drawing resurrection from the world's crucifixions. We pray 'Your kingdom come, your will be done on earth as it is in heaven'.

I have been freed for nearly seventy years from many of the duties of diocesan priests. True, some informed observers have suggested the duties might have been freed from me. But in the outcome, I have had scope to crisscross what seem to me converging tracks. These tracks seem to be leading Catholics, for one, and Christians at large, on a humble path with the rest of humanity to build from the earth a common home.

There is no need of a caveat on this book's limitations. They are clear. I offer only a few sticks of kindling for real firelighters coming along the way for the next seventy years.

A special aim of this book is to tell afresh the particular mission of Christian and Catholic laity within the great mission of humanity. It is the path of their clergy to accompany them and give them heart. The process of this book is to trace a few 'movement' projects. These began for me with a strong belief in everyday life as Catholics' vital mission. (This does not imply that other than Catholics were excluded, even in my schooldays. It was just that in the first few acts, history did not cast us together often.)

With Saint Paul, 'nearer now to our heavenly home than when we first learned to believe', I still see the mission of Catholics and all Christians as particular and particularly blessed. But so is the mission of every person and group. To hold one group blessed with their particular mission is not denying or denigrating the mission of others.

The reason for the unusual and possibly new word 'priesting' in the book's title is to keep its focus on new roles of the priest, in this case especially with new *movements or larger groups* of people. There is so much more to the life and mission of clergy than this book even attends to. It is meant as a small focus to serve the priesthood, ancient and modern, not replace it.

-.-.-.-.-.-.-.-.-.-.-.-.-.-.-.-.-.-.-.-

Even as a junior seminarian I was blessed to have encountered YCW (Young Christian Workers). That experience has stayed with me all my life as person and as priest, through all my sixty-seven years of 'priesting'.

The things I learnt from those teen years and write about here were simple yet profound. Mine has been like so many a faltering but never-ending journey following Jesus Christ, with my perspective progressing . . . from a rather limited Catholic setting to more that of Saint Paul, a cosmic Christ within all humanity.

- My reflective life began as an early teenager around a particular movement of young and dedicated Church members, by no means a stereotype, who were coming to an energising belief in the mission they shared with all young people, called to make a difference in every part of their life—work, family and community.
- This mission they believed was God-given, constituting the Church as a people of equally sacred roles, that of the priest distinct to be in a particular way with the people and for them.
- The importance of leaders alongside the priest. In YCW I saw people asked to take responsibilities among parish youth. For some this developed later as regional or national leadership in the Church. For all, life was opened as mutual leadership in their own worlds, whether small or large.
- Belonging to Church means belonging to all in their particular worlds.

Access to French provided me a richer Church world. It gave me perspectives beyond English-speaking accounts of priesting. I traced every available text in English by Fr Joseph Cardijn, the founder of YCW. He was for me the most powerful model of being a priest. He reinforced for me lay people having a personal mission and taking leadership, with the priest accompanying and supporting. I was introduced to a Church where people could see a connection between their faith and their life.

An identity check: although I have worked in parishes all my life, I have been only briefly a priest responsible for parishes. I have learnt that nothing grows in our Church without a critical number of priests. I was involved in various ministries, editor of the local Catholic newspaper, which meant working in a factory for years. I was university chaplain, then chaplain to lay movements of youth, students, family and neighbourhoods, with my responsibilities stretching from parish to international. This gave me flexibility to live in more worlds than I might have expected in a parish.

ATF Press: How is it that few priests seem to nurture lay people, to see the connection between faith and work in all aspects of their life?

PR Wilkinson: I think all priests want to be nurturing. But priests are often constrained by their fidelity to highly specified parish ministry. I hasten to add that many thousands of priests have had comparable review roles along the Church-world spectrum, especially in university and in pastoral roles beyond Church. My life beyond parish has often involved pastoral analysis and pastoral sociology.

Even the sacrament of reconciliation, 'Confession' as we called it, took several hours a week of a popular devotional routine. It embodied a fatherly role, greatly valued. It carried its own relationship of priest to people, an invaluable relationship but scarcely mutual. Priests and people often knew little of one another's lives. This is not deprecating this relationship, any more than recognising the similar relationship of doctor and patients in the past. But in both cases, it is to suggest a need to deepen and enrich traditional relationships.

My particular focus and passion has been encouraging leadership, reflecting with people in widely varied settings. Everyone has a unique experience of Church. In my case, halts have been as frequent as beginnings. So I am entitled to offer no more than pastoral opinions, however enthusiastically. 'Handsome is as handsome does' mothers have for generations told daughters with enthusiastic suitors, which applies equally to pastoral ideas. What matters is what works rather than what we have always done. rather than unexamined habits. 'The unexamined life is not worth living' is a maxim we attribute to Socrates on trial for impiety and corrupting youth. That he was subsequently sentenced to death wonderfully concentrates the mind.

I have been blessed with years of sharing systematic 'review of life', trying to keep in balance 'seeing, assessing, acting'. That has been with people one-to-one, in groups and in movements. The religion of the people was for centuries a well-populated round of services, private devotions and faithful lives. This has quite suddenly disappeared, certainly in its scale, but what has replaced it? Let's examine that more in these interviews.

Times are different, fewer people belong to a Church, or to its social groups. The numbers coming to Mass are fewer and fewer. Volunteering for non-religious scouts or service groups has suffered comparable declines.

ATF Press: So, what happened to the laity in the Catholic Church after Vatican II?

PR Wilkinson: The Vatican II document on the laity was not one that attracted much attention from the laity compared to the impact of the document on liturgy and that on the Church in the world. This latter dealt powerfully with world-scale issues but scarcely approached daily lives. Our Mass is now in English, with far greater participation by lay people. As well, there has been the rise of parish councils and notable lay roles at the diocesan level.

But the renewal of the lay person's life, what Cardijn called 'the lay, lay world', of home, work and society beyond Church affairs, has dwindled in people's faith awareness compared to that underway in many places pre-Vatican II. The *principle* of lay life as sacred is firmly held, but effectively *honouring* home life, work and community has faded. Ironically attention to life as a parish has blossomed among the few. Parish office and parish workers came into their own. These lay occupations were non-existent when I was ordained in the 1950s.

All these developments of lay roles within post-Vatican II parishes have been an unmixed blessing. They are not a pastoral problem. Nor is this a mealy-mouthed lip service. It is historically evident the Church cannot flourish with only clericals in clerical jobs.

Nonetheless, a vacuum exists in people's Christian awareness of the scope of the daily. Cardijn is yet to be discovered.

ATF Press: Did Cardijn have an influence on the Council document on the laity?

PR Wilkinson: He did, but not very publicly. Congar, renowned historian and theologian of Vatican II, makes it clear he expected more impact from Cardijn. But Congar understates how much the whole direction of the Council had been greatly influenced by Cardijn's life, ideas and work.

Somehow, a powerful popular model of laity as agents and subjects supporting one another in discovering their life as a mission, has not evolved.

To conclude this introduction, I anticipate the series of interviews ending. I am often asked if the Young Christian Workers Movement can be revived in Australia. I am sure individual groups can always be started and do great good. Maybe even a diocese could maintain a youth organisation following the methods and beliefs of YCW. But

Australian society lacks a self-aware workers movement and it lacks enough Catholic youth to make a genuine social movement that is young, Christian and worker. Vigorous social movements require a society that provokes them. Australian YCW flourished in a society that nourished it but no longer. We are too mixed up at present for a YCW.

But I end the book with the merest sketch of a movement I can imagine surpassing YCW in scope, vigour and depth.

The Young Christian Workers Movement of Europe was soon joined by movement of Young Farmers, Young Business, Young Fishers and others. YCW's belief in the sacred mission of every person in their own circumstances and their habit of reviewing their circumstances together ready to respond to the measure of an international social movement, proved transferable.

I believe the world waits for young Catholics and animators who bring that same conviction and discipline to create a world-wide movement of young Christian ecology activists. The name will be theirs to fashion. The tension between young workers' belief in themselves, and the neglect they suffered was what inspired the original YCW. Today, the greatest threat to human dignity is the threat of planetary destruction. This stands in stark contradiction to the Christian belief in self-respect and respect for the planet. This is the contradiction that can fire a distinct Christian world movement

I do little more than sketch such a movement to stir the imagination of young leaders and priests. The inevitable response to the suggestion of a Christian ecology movement is possibly a complaint. Would not such a movement be divisive? Why bring religion into it? Does not religion always start wars? And so on.

No doubt a less-than-helpful exclusive spirit could be imagined. But we have very effective and united Christian groups in every world movement. Red Cross began under a Christian symbol. Christian movements for peace are widespread. Christian groups for ecumenism are a gift to society and Church. Christian universities have been independently loyal to the cause of education. The ecology movement is widespread and benefits from its diverse expressions.

Catholic tradition offers a wealth of insights to the health of human ecology. A Christian youth movement for the environment would not have any interest in being divisive. A young ecologist who sensed divisive policies would walk away from them as false to the environment and religion.

'Think globally and act locally' was originally an environmental and town-planning dictum from 1915, the year YCW started. YCW showed that the vast energy of a global cause like the worker movement could be transformed into a way of life. YCW was inspired with pride, endurance, imagination and discipline by the worker cause and the cause of Christ. It transformed this energy and pride into lives that fitted a noble cause.

This gathering of a lifetime accompanying Christian movements that were open-hearted, but deep in faith and realism has convinced me that each generation has its own call. Anyone with whom I have shared these movements would see with delight that they could be surpassed by a new Christian youth movement to save the planet and humanity.

Maybe a line or a story from these humble accounts might spare reinventing the wheel for this century.

ATF Press: Do you have any reflections of the recent Australian Plenary Council?

PR Wilkinson: The Australian Council advanced the essential discussion of Church relationships among office holders in the Church. Questions of the public role of women in the Church, married priests, honouring First Nations Peoples, and sharing with other Churches are now open for development in a spirit of trust. How much the seven areas of attention will bear fruit waits to be seen. I was not closely involved but I have read little of mobilising a leadership among the people to the scale needed and possible.

We still wait for the world of *formation* to be addressed within the Church, a whole-of-life, life-long apprenticeship, a continual, gradual and mutual learning in being human and Christian. In a mutual apprenticeship model, the priest is still vital, a link, but now as one who also learns, who accompanies, who supports and contributes to a continuously richer and broader view of life, a bridge builder across Church and in society. Formation to me means a learning that is mutual, conscious, person-to-person. This means something like movements within the Church.

I have realised how much the power of the lay movements, which shaped my generation, was an apprenticeship. I remember the power of a young boy discovering the power to reunite with his dad by going to a film together. I remember the YCW girl picturing two candles on her desk, joining her work to her Mass. Without seeming pious, YCW leaders kept their eye out for those on the margins of their crowds. Somewhere there is always a movement of action/reflection-together waiting in the wings. When it does, it could be as powerful as the emergence of Catholic schools in the nineteenth century, of similar scale, turning out, not in.

Husbanding my few resources, I have expressly not addressed internal Catholic Churchmanship, issues like the exclusion of the female half of the Catholic Church from leadership as priests. Nor celibacy mandated for priests. Nor divorce and remarriage. Nor the rest of a century's worth of cultural issues of power and sexuality.

My focus is as limited as limitless, the middle distance. My songs and snatches are especially of the unChurched, searching to introduce an old Church to a new world. The currency of this discussion is social movements. To kidnap the words of former Prime Minister Julia Gillard about her record, the subject 'is not everything, but it is not nothing'.

Bob Wilkinson as a young boy

2

On the Road

ATF Press: Bob let's start with your early life.

PR Wilkinson: My childhood was very different from many. My parents had broken up in the early 1930's, leaving my mother for some years in precarious health. My earliest memories are of living with a foster family. I lived with a widow and her three grown daughters and a grown son. It was a loving and secure setting. I saw my mother relatively infrequently—whenever she could, she would come to visit me. I had four brothers and sisters at the Goodwood Orphanage. My oldest sister and brother were already at boarding schools, at Cabra and Sacred Heart College. This meant that I grew up, in effect, as an only child. I was with the foster family till I was six years of age. This did leave me with a generalised anxiety outside of a home setting. Yet I remember no sense of deprivation. I enjoyed and looked up to my mother and six siblings, the highlight of my childhood. My foster family stayed as friends all their life. My mother worked as a supervisor of a council playground.

My experience of the Church was much like that of any young person at that time. The Catholic Church was a strong enclave and you lived in a Catholic world. I remember once that I thought I had committed a mortal sin because I went to a friend's end-of- year Sunday School concert. I thought I was damning myself to hell for the sake of friendship. My experience of the faith was a stable and a secure one, but very personal and individual. Faith was not discussed; it was taught rather thoroughly but uninterestingly via the old Catechism. There was a strong sense of the uniqueness of the Catholic Church. The rest of the world was there presumably as a quarry to make Catholics out of. It certainly was not a very ecumenical view of the world.

ATF Press: Where did you go to school?

PR Wilkinson: I started at the Kingswood parish school, in the south of Adelaide, and then I moved to Saint Aloysius College run by the Sisters of Mercy, where two of my sisters were in secondary school there and I was at the parish primary school attached to their school. My mother had reunited us when I was in Grade 1, first in a single fronted three-room cottage in the inner city.

I must have been an unusually reflective child. I can remember in Grade 5 asking myself religious questions. I was not going to accept God rejecting those who were not Catholic and was rather pleased to read in the new Catechism of the time that sincerity would qualify everyone. It was Archbishop Beovich's own Catechism, benign its worldview.

Our family style of spirituality was very much a personal one. Being an altar boy in our family meant I got up each rostered morning for early Mass, woken by my mother. We had the family rosary each evening around the family table. We were a sane and normal Church-going family. At Mass we each had our own intentions to pray for. We stayed after Mass for our private thanksgiving, prayers, something of all the devotional elite. I felt no gap between my faith and my life as they fitted together quite naturally.

My mother was a qualified and highly regarded infant teacher and found work, first in the Catholic school system and then in the state school system.

My oldest brother and sister started working after matriculation. With their help my mother brought in enough to keep her seven children together. Then she rented from a generous aunt a comfortable bungalow in a well-to-do suburb, making for our middle-of-the-road existence in terms of education and social setting. My eldest brother joined the Royal Australian Air Force in the Second World War, followed by my second brother. The main influence in the house became my mother and my three sisters.

I met my father only once, for an hour. He had left South Australia after the separation, and we had no contact with or about him. He never had remarried. I was two years ordained a priest when I received a telegram from a priest in Hobart, who had known my parents, that he had come across my dad in the Repatriation Hospital in Hobart.

I flew straight there, picked up my brother living in Hobart at the time, and we proceeded to the Repat. My father was recovering well from lung surgery. He was pleased to see us, if laconic about it. But it was an Australian all-male chat quite laid-back for a first meeting in twenty-five years. I felt little from the encounter except identifying easily with him.

On our return the following day our world stopped. We were told, 'Your father died unexpectedly last night'.

When he heard this, Archbishop Young of Hobart convoked his priests to join me for Mass in the Cathedral for my father, a mark of respect for a priest of a diocese for one who has lost a parent. For this I have remained ever grateful.

I knew and know even now almost nothing about my father. Once an educated clerk, he died as an unskilled labourer on the hydro-scheme in Tasmania, aged fifty-five. My mother had never spoken ill of him, referring in passing only to his gifts spoiled by heavy drinking.

At Christian Brothers College from Grade 6 I remember hearing of vocations to the religious life and the priesthood. In my first year of secondary school I went to an interview with the seminary rector and put my name down as being interested.

My family shared an easy sense of 'duty plus generosity'. From early years, priesthood seemed to me not that attractive generous commitment, something I imagined might even be a question for me. Say, after university. However, in Second Year secondary, aged thirteen, after serving parish Mass one Sunday the visiting priest, rector of the seminary, asked me casually, 'Are you still interested in the seminary, son?' Somewhat academically, I answered 'Oh, yes'. On this, he replied matter-of-factly, 'we start in a fortnight'. Mentally shrugging at the logic I said, 'All right. A fortnight'. Neither the rector nor I had spoken to my mother.

And so it happened. Being fostered from earliest memory I was an independent soul. It did not occur to me to check my going to the seminary with anyone, even with my mother. To say she was surprised would be an understatement, the rest of the family refusing to believe it at first. But the attitude was favourable. After all, the minor seminary I entered at Third Year secondary was a glorified high school, not a locked down monastery. We came home every school holiday and worked in paying jobs. There was a free spirit about the place, and it was not heavily authoritarian.

In the seminary I met another student, Joe Grealy. Joe was a tradesman, a boilermaker, who had served his time as an apprentice at the Islington railway workshops in Adelaide. It was he who told me about this new parish youth group he belonged to which was called the Young Christian Workers (YCW). I was interested and impressed by his sense of responsibility and the idea that young people could have a sense of ownership, a sense of leadership in their own lives.

Joe and I started together in the minor seminary, he a year ahead of me. He had left school early to begin his apprenticeship as a boilermaker. Another one who was with us in the minor seminary, who came from the Port Pirie diocese was an electrician, Wes, who had been a Methodist before becoming a Catholic. He and Joe were at the minor seminary to acquire Latin before beginning philosophy, a three-year course entirely in Latin. Fortunately, I already had my high school years of Latin behind me.

With the two tradesmen, there were twenty of us still of school age in the minor seminary. Down the hill from us was philosophy house, an undergraduate institution. Minor House and Philosophy shared meals, sport and an easy social life.

Joe Grealy and I were five years apart in age, but we became good mates who also knocked around together in holidays. The friendship was to last a lifetime and introduced me to the world of industry and unions through his contacts.

My work over the long holidays was varied. I was a postman for a couple of years, and I worked behind the counter at the Myer department store in Adelaide for a couple of years. Then I was a mail messenger for the pastoral company Elder Smiths, running between Port Adelaide and the city office, taking a bus five times a day. I also stripped garden trees affected by fruit fly. My peak occupational rise was from second kitchen hand to conductor on the famous continental East-West train (now the Indian-Pacific).

Back to the seminary. We studied logic, psychology, cosmology, ethics, the philosophical question of the existence of God from the viewpoint of reason. It was equivalent to an undergraduate university course.

Because of my contact with Joe Grealey, I met and admired local and national YCW leaders. They were a lesson in themselves, confidently integrating their faith and life. They believed in in their role in the Church and at work. They had something that the seminary course did not have: relevance and engagement with life. In the YCW there was a strong sense that everyone had something to give. Experience mattered. I had not come across anything like it elsewhere.

At St Patricks theology seminary in Sydney, for the last four years of training for priesthood I recognised something significant about students with YCW involvement. The YCW was not present in Sydney. The role of the laity was not as front and foremost in this Sydney seminary as it had been in most other parts of Australia. This resulted in a radical and profound difference in how students saw the laity and the priesthood. I was more aware of my formation from the YCW than in the more formal seminary training I had in Sydney. The YCW offered a more vital and integrated spirituality within my view of priesthood.

The seminary course in Sydney was a classical course: dogmatic theology, moral theology, Church history, canon law, scripture etc. It could have been much the same course from the fourteenth century; a timeless course. It was adequate but not dynamic. The rector had no idea of bringing in speakers from outside. We even had a struggle to get access to the *Sydney Morning Herald*.

There were about 100 students from various parts of Australia at Manly seminary at that time. There was certainly nothing precious about the whole community. I was very aware I was following two parallel courses. One the formal, the other my informal YCW education. I would visit the YCW headquarters in Melbourne with its leadership as aware of themselves as leaders as we were in the seminary.

Because of the 'See, Judge, Act', method they were geared to young people being alert to what was happening to them, those around them and to each other. Back in the seminary, I was a good student but continued to read very widely in lay apostolate matters. By the time I was ordained I was reading French. I found France and Belgium especially looking in more depth at the experiences of young people around the world. Suhard, a Cardinal a Paris, was the author of *Rise or Decline of the Church*, addressing questions that confronted the universal Church, that is, the impact of industrial society. The alienation of the working class from the Church was the central pastoral issue.

Socially conscious Australian Catholics had been studying issues of the Great Depression of the 30's, leading the Australian Catholic Bishops in 1936 to institute a national office for 'Catholic Action'. This was not aimed at partisan politics, but a commitment to social justice, disposing numbers in Australia to learn about this YCW International, founded in Europe in 1927.

One book, available only in French very sadly, was the extremely comprehensive text for YCW leaders. Its title translates as the *Yeast in the Dough*. Originally published as five booklets of page-a-day examples, it covered hundreds of topics from work, home and society. It was very well-illustrated with pictures and text, very attractive printing and preparation. It had a highly developed lay spirituality to a degree that I had never encountered till then (and still haven't). Written by Paris YCW chaplain Fr Henri Godin, later a key figure in the French priest-worker movement in France. It showed me new possibilities of living faith.

Books on Cardijn, and his own addresses as *Layman into Action*, were appearing in English from the 1950s and were widely read within YCW. I assumed many priests would have had access to the French literature but, in reality, Fr JF Kelly of Melbourne may have been the only other priest at the time trying to assimilate the same European thinking.

Both as a way of life and method of formation, the 'see, judge, act' mentality has stayed with me at least as a striving. Regarding that famous formula, it may help to note that 'see' is not the same as simply 'anything of interest?' but rather 'any experience that concerns us?', that 'judge' does not mean 'be judgmental' but something quite opposite, 'does what we see concern us enough to take some action', and 'act' is more than a discussion topic, rather 'what someone is doing to make a difference'. Its inspiration is that lightning a candle is better than cursing the darkness. Everyone agrees that 'see-judge-act' sounds useful: fewer agree that it is the essential habit for becoming human.

ATF Press: Bob, thank you for this continuing unfolding of your life and work. It is clear that there are strong strands developing of how you have worked as a priest over the years. Cardijn has indeed been a big influence from before you were ordained and, as we will see in these interviews, the Jocist tradition has remained a constant. We will look next time at your early period of priesthood, the sort of things you were doing, your work with the YCW in Adelaide.

Bob as a seminarian in Adelaide in the 1950s. Bob is in the third row, second from the right

Bob Wilkinson giving his first blessing to his mother at his ordination in Adelaide.

3

Parish Encounter

ATF Press: Let's begin with the time after your ordination.

PR Wilkinson: I think one of the most powerful influences at that stage, just ordained twenty to twenty-five-year-olds, had been meeting national and some South Australian leaders in the YCW, but with their particular maturity, normality and of linking faith and life. They had real interest in other young people and it was an experience of the Catholic Church beyond seminary training and with it a lack of interest in current realities.

I was an enthusiastic parish YCW chaplain from the beginning. I had the good fortune to meet two outstanding leaders in large YCW groups in my first parish. One of them was on the national executive of the later YCW Girls movement and the other a future union leader. There were five to ten leaders of some fifty boys and fifty girls. There was the general meeting, sports and musicals in the parish hall. For me the most powerful time was spending an hour each week with the young boy and girl who were preparing the gospel reflection for their leaders' meetings. So, it was an hour each week listening to each of them speak about their week, their home life, their work and their life in general. I was meeting with the two parish presidents every week.

It was a fairly intense chaplain's work. I do not know how many chaplains had such intense communication with their parish youth. I became deeply immersed in the circumstances of those young workers. The parish I was in, Semaphore, was then in the 1950s an industrial, totally working-class parish.

It was a great experience for almost four years, with annual national meetings where I became gradually aware of the national YCW. This became the most vital framework of my priesthood. The central principles of YCW presented implications for adults.

The YCW was not politically significant, but it was in touch with the lives of young people and was conspicuous by its spirit of community.

It was a different age of the Catholic Church. Until 1970 the Australian Catholic Church was at its most historically vigorous. Every year four or five priests were ordained to the priesthood in the late 1950s. Three out of four Catholics attended Sunday Mass. It is now less than one in two. There was a trace of release from being an embattled group who had to struggle for existence. One or two went to university in those days. There were many intellectually gifted people who in later years would have gone on to university who were very attached to parish, and only a few people had cars. The parish was very Catholic, very local, very gifted, very confident.

ATF Press: How did those local YCW groups understand themselves as participating in the life of the Church in the 1950s?

PR Wilkinson: They experienced the strength and the weakness of the Australian scene. It was the local youth group but they knew they were part of a national YCW structure and because of that had a certain status in the Church. The YCW employed their first full-time worker in the 1950s.

ATF Press: How did they see themselves as part of something bigger?

PR Wilkinson: First through interstate football matches. There was a policy of making YCW National Council each year in a different city. At my first meetings, leaders discussed their meetings. Maybe ten young people from twenty-five Catholic Church dioceses around the country attended. Contact with international YCW was slight, although we all knew there was such a thing. In 1958 they welcomed to Australia, Father Joseph Cardijn as their movement's hero. I wrote the script for a youth gathering at the Adelaide seminary depicting youth and YCW in every continent. I found later that earned me the editors post in our *The Southern Cross* diocesan paper. It was a script of an account of YCW on six full stages. In 1960 the National Catholic Girls Movement joined with the boys and became the one YCW.

ATF Press: What was seen as the role of the priest chaplain in those days?

PR Wilkinson: The main thing was for him to be interested. There were two levels to that. There were chaplains who encouraged the group and showed up at meetings. There was another level of people who would meet to reflect more seriously on the role of the priest. There had been no systematic thought. In 1960 a new national chaplain Fr Brian Burke, arrived. He had been the local Melbourne chaplain. He later became international chaplain.

At the time the new national president and executive developed YCW 'action' campaigns. The first one that I recall was on street lighting/safety. It was the first time that groups started looking beyond the Church and parish. Groups went to local district council's and these responded to the issue of street lighting/safety. This led to a fresh campaign, issues like family life and safe driving. Involvement in international YCW meetings developed more mature reflection on Church and society. The Vietnam War introduced serious political conflict in the YCW.

ATF Press: Was the YCW seen as just a social group of Catholics who came together who were Catholic?

PR Wilkinson: That calls for impressions. Parishes varied, but a spirit was evident. Young people saw YCW bringing responsibility for each other. Bishops saw them as very effective leaders in the Catholic Church. It encouraged ideals of work, and life and that was a powerful experience. There was little action beyond a youth organisation. But to look at them as solely social groups would underestimate them. The life of the young was the focal point. The Catholic was so strong on identity it scarcely needed promoting. Being Catholic was like being Australian.

ATF Press: How much influence was there from the national group on the local group or the state body?

PR Wilkinson: It was pretty constant. They had national visits to each state by leaders all under twenty-five and drawn from each state. YCW differed from a social group by its growing sense of responsibility for the young themselves by the young. The work had always been seen as 'to serve, educate and represent' young workers. That's how they saw themselves. Training days were held regularly for and by under twenty-fives. This differed from the Sydney model whose youth organisers could be people in their fifties. The rest of

Australia had developed from of a European model with a vigorous reputation for being young people by young people for young people. It had a sense of itself strongly connected to the Church but open to the whole of life. The relationship with the Church was so organic it was scarcely an issue, it was simply the young Catholic Church in action. The YCW started at the end of the Depression in the late 1930s at a time of social awareness. It was simply the young Catholic Church in action, a blue-print of peoples struggles for better things.

ATF Press: Was there ever any thought of diverse groups in Australia, say like the French Catholic Church?

PR Wilkinson: No, not really. The French had bigger numbers to deal with, an extensive and intensive culture. They inherited a working class with a weak Catholic identity. YCW mobilised as much more a class movement. YCW led to a rural movement and then to one for fishermen and another for business. Italy had a Catholic Action model for youth as part of the whole parish, politically organised against the communists and socialists. Priests were prominent organisers.

Bob Wilkinson at his first Mass

ATF Press: Was the review of life method used here in Australia?

PR Wilkinson: Yes, the student version of YCW, the Young Christian Students movement meetings originally had its 'Items of Interest' and 'Facts of Action', rather random and unreflective daily responses to encourage a see-judge-act spirit. Later more thoughtful leaders did emerge who took review of life to university with them.

ATF Press: When you were in your first parish in the 1950s did you have any contact with the YCS groups there?

PR Wilkinson: Yes, they were totally school orientated and integrated into the school. Most Catholic secondary schools had a YCS group and it would have been almost totally run by the school, with a religious sister or brother responsible. There was the genuine element of students holding office, exercised at a simple level until the 1970s. Some moved on to the YCW from their leadership in YCS and identified more maturely with the Catholic Church because of that. At a religious level it helped young people think about their faith. It was the early student space, however docile.

ATF Press: It would have been normal for a young person to be in YCW group in the parish?

PR Wilkinson: It would have been exceptional for a young person in a parish not to at least be on the edges of the YCW group. It is worth noting that the YCW defended its autonomy in refusing to become a youth wing of Bob Santamaria's political projects.

ATF Press: Where was your own thinking and reading going at this time when you were involved in the parish work?

PR Wilkinson: Local reading on the laity was scarce. There were some books and publications on YCW groups and the mission and vocation of young people. From Fr Brian Burke there was a strong emphasis that the YCW was the young person's group, not the priest's. He hammered me that 'It is not your YCW, it belongs to the young workers'. So many of the priests grew up with young people as their colleagues and were about the same age as the young people. Potentially it was radical but as an organisation sounding radical ideas came in the late 1960s. The capacity of the young person for reflection and their seriousness for concern for others, were models for the priests. There was no tradition of conflict or of roles but rather loyalty between priests and people that immigrated from the United Kingdom and the Irish Church. When Vatican II came in the 1960s it seemed simply to fill in the dotted lines of matters in harmony with spirit of the YCW.

ATF Press: In your early time as a priest before the Vatican Council how did you see the Catholic Church and how did you see the priesthood?

PR Wilkinson: It was a conflict-free world. I now see that as a pity. I saw the priest was there to help young people in their life and their mission and that altered the balance of power. Young people knowing they are being treated as colleagues.

ATF Press: What was the view of the Catholic Church in the 1950s and early 1960s.

PR Wilkinson: There was almost no reflection on the life of Church as such. It was a given. As the fish in the pond do not notice the water in the pond, the life of Catholics was very much within the Church. It comprised much of their world, and they felt blessed to belong. There was a sense of being an established Church. There was a confidence of the young. At national meetings, priests were discouraged from talking too much. Cardijn did not elaborate much about the Church as it was so much a fact in Catholic countries. The role and the dignity of the person in their own lives was paramount and Church implications are still works in progress. Cadijn argued that the role of the laity was totally united with the role of the clergy, in harmony but distinct from it.

In 1972 as part-time national chaplain to the YCS I began to appreciate that there were genuine challenges, even contradicted in the Church, many points to be contested in the Church. Differences, tension, even division, now emerged among young Catholics as among all youth. The days of singing together as choir were over.

ATF Press: Next time we will look at the Vatican II period and where change occurred in the lay movements leading to the 1970s. From this interview, it is clear that the 1970s was a time when the vigorous unified life of the youth movements disappeared over about a year. Their leadership became radicals of Church and society. In the whole of society the young were disengaging from the past. These will be interesting issues to talk about and tease out some more! Thank you!

Bob Wilkinson's three sisters, from left to right: Betty, Moira, & Phil.

Bob Wilkinson with Joseph Cardijn in Adelaide, 1958

4

'Stop the Press'

ATF Press: Let's start with the time after Vatican II. You have finished your seminary training and you have been in a parish and then you became editor of the local Catholic newspaper, *The Southern Cross.*

PR Wilkinson: Let's go back a bit first. I have realised how important publishers were for me in my life. Without the likes of publishers Sheed and Ward I would have seen only a youth group. Their books, and the French literature, expanded my horizons.

Stages in my awareness and development are clear now. When I first came across the YCW it was the idea of an organisation for young people that drew me, rather than what I grew to see as a movement that bridged the gap between faith and life. It was first meeting Joe Grealy, a YCW leader before his seminary days, and the YCW program which appealed to me. One of the things I realised was the skill of YCW organisation. Someone might come down from the diocesan YCW office to our parish. We took it for granted at the time, but the fact that there was some leadership and advice from the diocese shifted our way of thinking. We were not just local groups, but part of something bigger. This affected my view of the Church. By standing back I saw something bigger. Standing back was seeing that what was happening in my parish was also happening in other parishes. I had the chance to see things in a national perspective from making my way to the national YCW councils. That again introduced me to a wider perspective on the whole country, a national Church and society, one in which the world of young people had a place, even though I might not have used the same concepts. I spent my holidays, soon after I was ordained, with YCW country groups in Bendigo, Victoria.

To push this a little further, there were two things about our parish YCW.

First, there was a program that came out from the National Office. It was never very exciting. There were articles in it which we scarcely read, but the leaders met, took minutes, and shared 'items of interest and facts of action'. This was an open-ended discussion of the past week. The experience of young people as leaders, named as such, aiming to care for other young people.

Second, there was the wisdom of YCW providing 'supplementary training weekends' where there would be more sustained discussion. It was a growing awareness on several fronts of young people bridging the gap between faith and life. I almost took for granted that there were young people close to my age who were thinking about and acting out of their faith. It was not something that they could have been taught at school, it was something that they had learnt through the best experience could offer.

Unlike Christine Doctrine at school, this agenda was owned and developed by leaders. Everyone's experience was respected.

I remember a young girl saying that she imagined her desk at work as an altar with candles on it to see her work as her offering at Mass. Another spoke of standing at traffic lights and seeing every person there with a special purpose from God. I took it for granted, the world of YCW, but it was creating a new culture. This culture incorporated the earlier classroom teaching, but it also rendered their personal experience something shared and valuable by the attention it was given.

Growth or Decline, a pastoral letter, and later a book, by Cardinal Suhard in Paris at the end of WW ll gave an account of French society, shining a light on the Catholic Church and the people, without moralising. He was talking about what had been known since the nineteenth century as 'the social question', the fate of the working class. Industrial cities were growing without the Church. Churchs might still be full, with enough to keep priests busy. But the working-class was more and more alienated.

Before WW ll each year a *Social Week* took place in France, on a different theme, bringing together the best minds in the country looking at faith and life, building up analysis of society, of Church and faith. Reading summaries of these introduced me to a world, one beyond Australia, an active world of people engaged with a 'see, judge act' method. I was being introduced into sociology, a scene, a world, a kind of dreaming that was already global.

Father Brian Burke was one of the few I encountered with a sociological perspective. He drew me from any clericalist position to broader questions. 'Why' and 'How' were the questions.

There was a popular novel, *Fishers of Men,* which was very readable, by another Belgian, van Meert. This was a fictional account of a YCW lad. It carried no theory and was worth a dozen lectures. Cardijn's *Young Worker Faces Life* and *Layman Into Action* were probably the first books which many YCW leaders would read. In each diocese there was a 'back and forth'. Leaders in parishes who showed promise were invited to the diocesan level, the most gifted identified as 'key leaders', all by young people.

From the beginning this was a movement of young people, for young people, by young people. Chaplains could speak but they could not vote at National Councils. Priests were supporting the laity in their apostolate, almost the reverse of the 'Catholic Action' definition. YCW, well before Vatican II, modelled the participation of the priest in the apostolate of the laity. Thus, for many YCW priests and leaders, Vatican II's attention to the people seemed already self-evident.

In Australia, until Whitlam's 1970s era tertiary education was much less available than now. In a working-class district like my first parish, I knew one graduate, a primary teacher. There were Catholic dentists, lawyers, doctors, but they stood-out as elite. Leaders in the YCW, were capable and gifted thinkers, responding quickly to the vision of the YCW. These days they would have been graduates.

ATF Press: For you, which were the most important documents of Vatican II?

PR Wilkinson: For me, obviously the ones which deal with the laity and the Church in the world stood out. That said, I was constantly searching, but never found in Vatican ll documents, anything expanding structurally the mission of the person in their circumstance of home, work and leisure. The Council certainly honoured the laity, but the emphasis was more on laity within Church, drawing attention away from the role of the laity in the whole of life: Doing good in Church life caused collateral damage in daily life. The Council moved us to recognise people's participation in worship, but ironically it did not follow through to look at their lives. The document on the

Church in the Modern World was excellent, but it dealt with large-scale issues. It spoke to those with an interest in social analysis. Despite a memorable opening statement that the hopes and fears, the joys and sorrows of the people are those of the Church, no method of sharing these developed beyond a recognition of See, Judge, Act as a pastoral method.

Paris in 1968 symbolised a vast and complete social revolution. The Vatican Council was a great development of the previous Church, but it sometimes happens that the Church develops a new role in a society just as that form of society is being replaced by another.

The years immediately after the Council, the years 1965 to 1970, were still a period of flourishing and were the most vigorous of the YCW everywhere. For me, the peak year was the National Council of 1968 at Broken Hill. It was harmonious, vigorous: the leaders were very competent choosing relevant campaign topics. Full-time workers from Asia brought new perspectives on social activism. At the same time, the ground was moving under our feet, young people were changing. The Church was all dressed up and ready to go, just as the party moved off and you had the world of the 1970s. 'Long haired lay-abouts' were discernible to people as rarely Church goers.

The YCW was several things at this time. At the national level, there was confusion between radical views. The national leaders and chaplains were very involved in the Vietnam Moratorium Movement, aiming to halt Australia's involvement action. Around the world, in military dictatorships, YCW leaders had paid with their lives. National YCW leaders in Australia became impatient with the everydayness of the YCW here.

Full-time leaders could see great room for a more radical people's movement, but around Australia the general membership started to drop from thousands to dozens, in the search for authenticity.

The past was cut adrift by the young everywhere in an irreversible tectonic shift. People who had worked hard getting a parish YCW group going, running a football group, going to Sunday Mass did not have clear ideas of international questions. A section of experienced YCW and YCS leaders could find parish level rather tame, and were almost scandalised by people just going to Mass and maintaining the parish. For these young there was not enough questioning. Many abandoned Catholic Church practice because it did not meet their expectations. Young people in many Christian denominations were no longer interested in the Church itself. For many young Catholics even the work of the Vatican Council left them untouched. There is a key demographic note here. The sudden rupture of 1968 did not cause a rupture of post-school youth moving on to Church practice, but more exactly it started a decline in teenagers moving into the Church as adults.

Structurally, from about 1968 the number of people who were socialised into the Church, slowed, not matching the population growth. It was gradual enough that priests who worked in parishes did not notice a great change. Churches were still full, and the Church was vigorous. There were Church vocations, but the trajectory of decline was growing, it was clearly there. Church attendances did not reach a reversal until the early nineties, twenty years later.

Among Catholics born before 1950 Church was still active.

In Adelaide, you had the development of the Christian Life Movement, an adult movement which was home-grown. In every parish you had ex-YCWs, who were keen to develop this vigorous movement of lay people. You had parish clergy sympathetic. The diocese supported a full-time CLM team of four, with groups in most city parishes, groups of five or six couples responding to friendliness of the shared review of life. Morphet Vale had twenty groups at one time, over the 70s a thousand young married couples who thrived on Vatican II.

Masses were still full, but numbers were not being renewed. The equivalent was happening far beyond Church in society. Young people were not joining scout groups, not the Freemasons, or other service groups like Rotary. All volunteer groups gradually declined in numbers.

Sociology suggests that enough radical change in technology can lead to a new dominant class. With the digital age you had the rise of such a new class, particularly in communications. What became the reality of young people was foreign to the official Church. We still had men being trained as priests over seven years to be preachers, though the young were not listening to sermons. Many of those who were still in the Church were showing almost a pre-Vatican taste in liturgy, theology and the relationship between the clergy and people, identifying almost as a fortress besieged by a spiritually lost society.

Here arises a testing question. Let it be declared dishonest for any reader to interpret the question that follows as destructive or negative. It is about something to be added, not replaced.

Is there, then, a major oversight in the investment of Australian Catholic pastoral energy. Have we witnessed (or failed to witness) collateral damage from the growth of such excellent professional Catholic education, from school to post-graduate, over the last fifty years?

We have scarcely examined, over those last fifty years, whether institutions, texts and courses have so merited Church attention that nothing comparable in resources and thinking has gone into the 'apprenticeship model' of faith formation that voluntary lay movements once offered.

The hypothesis needs careful stating. The issue is not with formal education. The development of widespread Catholic schools, along with professional undergraduate and graduate education is an untrammelled gift. The Church would be injured by any subversion of our formal education.

But there are two kinds of formation, formal and informal; each needs the other. In Economic terms they are not fungible, in that one cannot replace the other. Formal education is marked by professional teachers, education systems, with courses and topics, with experts who teach in institutions. Even recognising that formal education may not always be perfect, it is necessary. Without it, the Church would be adrift in modern society.

But the problem is that *informal* education (shorthanded neutrally in what follows as 'formation' to distinguish it from formal 'education') has not matched its formal partner.

Formation relies even more on personal relationships than education. Informal education has declined since Vatican II. We need structures and processes that are more tailored experience. Those involved in formation are required totally to listen and dialogue. Formal education is the better for having these characteristics and may not even be entertained without them. But courses and classes have an objectivity that makes them less totally dependent on personal relationships.

The 'see, judge, act' process in some form is the normal way to develop formation. The enquiry method is valued by formal education and has become a mainstay of much education. But in formal education, the enquiry method serves the subject of the course. The agenda of informal formation finds its unity, not in a subject or issue, but in the complex life of the participants. No doubt, further finessing is possible, but there is no question the mutual apprenticeship of formation is distinct from education, not separated but distinct. In formation as understood here, relationships are its life; there is none without ongoing personal commitment to ongoing personal community relationships.

ATF Press: I think the informal process is key to how you have lived and worked as a priest. What Influence did Vatican II have on you personally?

PR Wilkinson: In many ways it was formalising what I had encountered in the Cardijn movements. The liturgy was a new insight, the insight how much more liturgy could be active, conscious and shared.

Certainly, I was blessed as editor of *The Southern Cross* in Adelaide with bishops who trusted me. In my ten years with the local Catholic newspaper, I was never once called to account or rebuked by the bishop for whatever line I had taken in *The Southern Cross*, even in the delicate debates surrounding contraception. I was loyal to policies of the bishop but I was left to write and to take responsibility which was not the case in some other parts of Australia or around the world. I have no doubt I warranted interventions from less tolerant owners.

ATF Press: How did the changes evident in the Church documents affect your thinking when you were editor?

PR Wilkinson: There was a whole new framework of how to see things.

Almost every feature of modern life was a source for Vatican II.

Thanks to Cardijn, I have always seen my role as a priest to encourage people in their own lives. The Council reinforced that. If the priest has a strong belief in people's lives, as an act of faith, simply to be with people, accompanying them, is formative for priest and people.

I saw an example of accompanying people in Sr Ruth Egar RSM working in the Morphett Vale parish. She simply visited people where they lived, in their houses. People asked, 'Why are you coming, what help are you looking for?'. She was formed in Cardijn's faith in daily life.

She said, 'I want to know more about your life'. Through her interest in what was happening to them, couples took to her suggestion of sharing as families in CLM. Up and down every street, in workplaces, in parish groups she developed over a ten-year period, couples who started to see creative scope and a new sense of ownership of their own lives and of their Church.

ATF Press: The radicalisation of society and of the Cardijn movements has meant that they have become other than what they were in the 1940s and 1950s. Can you please talk a little more about that?

PR Wilkinson: It is hard to know where society is. But in one point it is easy to say what it is not. Society today has profoundly rejected faith in the past as binding. We are expected to test all old habits by experience. Politics reflects at present a confusion about society when one looks at world leaders. The Church still searches for a way to integrate its age-old definitive teaching style into the new society.

The Church is well integrated in some migrant and refugee support groups, such as the Vietnamese, Indian and Filipino cultures. The Church has not had much success integrating itself in Australian culture at large except in its large institutions of education, health and welfare. I hope that our reflection here can add to the search for a convincing pastoral culture.

The Catholic Church is strong in the services it provides. Catholic schools, health care and social services are highly regarded all over Australia, but service provision has almost become the tail that wags the Catholic dog. Two generations of people who have sent their children to Catholic schools have often escaped any personal Catholic culture and show little sign of wanting it.

The Catholic Church has changed greatly for the better, but the world in which it swims no longer recognises it, the world does not acknowledge Church as vital. It is a private enthusiasm with highly valued outcomes. In issues surrounding life's beginning and end, abortion and euthanasia, the Catholic Church is proudly distinct.

Many including Catholic Australians do not share the Catholic Church's absolute defence of innocent life. Above all, the exclusion of women from senior Church roles of authority has simply lost the sympathy of girls and women at large and a majority of men too. Conservatives have been so active defending traditional leadership models, they have missed the price in disgust that the Church pays for the debate.

The Church's rejection of gay marriage, and the way it has done it, has quite simply alienated many young Australians. Its rejection of artificial contraception is regarded as an eccentricity by most Australians including Catholics. Young Catholic say, 'we will use our own conscience, thanks'. Once the model of Church authority was questioned in such a vital reality as family planning, the remaining authority seems to be shrinking. The Church itself has been rejected. This is not to debate the issues. This is the course of history, for better or worse.

ATF Press: Thank you Bob, for yet another interesting look at your life as a priest and once again teasing out elements of what you see as a new vision of 'priesting'. Our next conversation will focus more on your time with YCW.

NCGM (National Catholic Girls Movement) national meeting.
Bob Wilkinson is on the far-right front row

5

Young Christian Workers

ATF Press: Let us look at what you had learned from the YCW and then in a later interview we will look at the YCS.

PR Wilkinson: I have realised how much unheralded, and I think unanalysed, the Australian YCW has been up to say the 1960's. It was not a social movement in its scale. The usual scale of a social movement is one that changes society. Up to that stage the Catholic Church in Australia had been quite a strong society in itself. It was a strong cultural group that influenced all aspects of life. The YCW exercised a profound change in the relationships of clergy and laity at that time for three reasons.

First, the method of structuring the YCW was to name 'leaders', chosen as proactive leader's others would accept. The very fact of naming and positioning a person, lay people as leaders was significant.

The second thing was marked, and it was the central emphasis on life beyond Church. Young people at home, work and leisure. The whole emphasis was on the dignity and worth of every lay person and the invitation to make a difference already in any young person's life. In YCW, 'mission' was never seen as taking on something more. The mission was already their life.

Third, it was a group for young people, led by young people and there were no priests in a director's role. I remember the Sydney's Catholic Youth Organisation, being staffed by middle aged people in their headquarters. In Adelaide there was a massive number of young YCW priests similar in age to the young people. There was a new relationship—the priest's role was seen as accompanying the leaders rather than directing. From 1945 to 1965 the relationship of priests and leader was friendship. It was a major social change in the Church itself. The paternalisation was much less marked than traditionally. This was scarcely exclusive to YCW but nowhere else was this a set purpose.[1]

The priest founder of YCW in Australia was Fr Frank Lombard of Melbourne. He lived Cardijn's vision to promote and insist on lay leadership. Normally nobody over twenty-five years of age stayed, even in positions of leadership. The priests and bishops dealt with a whole new reality of a self-aware youth body of YCW. Some dioceses funded the full-timers. And the Bishops funded the National Office, hands-off after the funding was given. The bishops did not look for involvement in politics. Vietnamese bishops made their political hopes clear.

ATF Press: Members of YCW groups would have been industrial workers?

PR Wilkinson: The boys were often in blue-collar jobs, the girls more in white-collar jobs. Until the 1970s there was little tertiary education in Australia. It meant you had a supply of leaders who would go on to university, but then could not. There in YCW you had a very capable leadership group. In the girl's groups there were hairdressers, office workers. There were few factory workers among the girls. It reflected the absence of industrial working women in the parishes, more than of boys and men.

Members of the leader's groups paid a small membership fee at each meeting. The program for the meetings came from the National Office for a fairly formalised meeting. From the 1950's on it was a fairly formalised meeting. There was not a vigorous questioning of society, but there was a very real spirit of friendship and contacts. YCW understood the message that the life of every young worker was important. There were leaders' meetings weekly and a general meeting fortnightly open to all young people. There was careful reflection at the leader's review to see no one had been neglected, a very pleasant leadership by friendship that was quite thorough in its methods. The general meeting had some sort of entertainment, with an opening prayer, and then a talk or music. Till the 1970s boys and

---

1. Later the girl's movement changed from NCGM (National Catholic Girls Movement) to YCW, but boys and girls YCW kept their separate administration until 1970.

the girl's meetings were separate with possibly up to about fifty at general meetings. There was a strong emphasis on keeping in touch with one another between meetings. The mentality was outward looking. But we must remember that the only transport till the 1960s was by push-bike, so district was the world, except for tram trips.

There were six or so at a leader's meeting which was led by a president. It was usually an informal group. The priest, the chaplain, would see each president once a week for an hour just talking about life. The priest spent time with other leaders regularly preparing the gospel discussion. All this was as much an education for the priest in the life of young people. The National Office later in the 1960s began to encourage local groups to develop their own campaigns on local issues. Each leader in turn had the chance to share their week. The sense was of equal dignity, without conflict.

Most parishes in Adelaide had a YCW group, noted for their vigour, parishes were pleased to have them. There was a young curate in most parishes, young priests in their twenties. Almost instinctively most worked with the YCW group.

Many parishes took part in YCW football and basketball competitions, popular events.

The emphasis was home, work and leisure.

ATF Press: What were the effects of Vatican II?

PR Wilkinson: Vatican II moved the emphasis to the role of the laity *within* the Church, just as the young people were drifting to a new culture averse to the past. That had not been the role of the YCW, which had a focus on the role of lay people in their own life. Vatican II somehow replaced the YCW and its focus from the laity as the 'lay, lay life' to use another phrase from Cardijn. The change in emphasis due to the Council came with the revolution of the 60s, the sexual revolution and the rejection of almost anything traditional. Fewer and fewer young people were socialised into the life of the Church.

Archbishop Gleeson of Adelaide, Brian Moylan and Monsignor Cardijn in Adelaide in 1958

6
All in the Family

ATF Press: What was the birth control debate like for a Catholic newspaper editor?

PR Wilkinson: Let me divert slightly here and talk again about my time as editor of the local Catholic paper, *The Southern Cross*. In 1969 priests began to seek new links with one another. It was a year after the Pope Paul VI's *Humanae Vitae* on birth control. Archbishop of Hobart, Guilford Young, teased me by saying that I had dodged this in *The Southern Cross*. I had said that no one could identify with authorised Catholic teaching while promoting artificial contraception. To me the word 'authorised' opened thought of conscience in the life of Catholics.

Among Catholics birth control became a matter for individual conscience. In *The Southern Cross* we freely published correspondence about the sensitive issues of birth control. There were never any constraints put on the Catholic Press in Adelaide by the archbishop and I was left to my own devices as editor with responsibility for content.

ATF Press: Was it difficult to keep a position in editorials?

PR Wilkinson: No, not at all. They were very confident years. The Catholic tradition requires people to follow their conscience. Until now, consciences accepted official teaching. Now came confusion. I have read that a million people left the Catholic Church in Australia over the issue. Many took their own position. They had the freedom to express their opinions, something I defended very strongly. In Adelaide there was little bitterness in the birth control debate.

The hottest debate at that time concerned the Vietnam War. An historian has told me that I was the first person in the Church in Australia to support a halt to fighting, a moratorium. Bob Santamaria launched a full-page challenge to me in the Melbourne Catholic *Advocate.*

ATF Press: Can we look now at your years with Adelaide's Christian Life Movement

PR Wilkinson: In the 1970s I worked with the Christian Life Movement (CLM), Adelaide's home-grown family movement, a very vigorous movement in its own right.

It has struck me that there were different *grades* of Church movements. CLM was a nonpolitical group based on a very strong sense of community, and it was distinct. It became a highly developed network in the city parishes of Adelaide, some having a number of groups. I do not know of any other place in Australia where Vatican II developed such an outreach. It was not a movement as developed as the feminist movement, or gay rights movements, which were seeking society-wide change. CLM was a more modest movement within the Catholic Church in Adelaide, a volunteer based linking where people could see that they made a difference in their own lives, beyond the personal. It had personal emphasis, exercised in community.

ATF Press: How did CLM start?

PR Wilkinson: CLM came from the Newman Institute, adult education work of the diocese and followed fairly explicitly YCW 'See, Judge, Act', methods. Parish halls to 'cottage groups' in homes that progressively adapted the theme of personal mission.

I became diocesan chaplain in 1970, supporting the secretary, Brian Moylan, an ex national YCW full-time worker. We might have had some fifty groups in Adelaide, a number in some parishes. The diocese funded a team of four leaders.

In the Morphet Vale area of Adelaide, a new housing area, CLM diocesan worker, Sister Ruth Egar RSM, served as an organiser. Its eventual twenty groups were a strong religious movement based on review of life, like YCW, with a constant reflection on a gospel passage. Personal spirituality was expressed as local parish community. CLM worked with other Churches, with the SA Housing Trust and the Noarlunga Medical Centre's groups supporting neglected housing estates. Neighbourhood groups developed in this phase, inspired Sister Ruth to insist on total parish involvement in Basic Ecclesial Communities in the 1900s.

The Christian Life Movement paralleled the Teams of Our Lady, another lay movement international in nature and not parish centred. Teams were geared towards a more tertiary-educated adult family base. CLM was of Adelaide origin, Teams was an international movement founded in France after World War II. The Teams being international still exist unlike the CLM. CLM had a sense of being in the tradition of Cardijn movements, with many of its members ex YCW. The CLM was supported by the Adelaide Archdiocese as a diocesan movement employing a diocesan team. The Teams were independent. Their international character offered a national identity that is still strong. The high number of graduates found a congenial setting. Working as chaplain with both CLM and Teams I found both movements matched in the strong bonds around family. I found in both movements a rich home.

CLM declined in the 1980s in the number of groups. This coincided with the return of women to the workforce. CLM had been largely based on a network of women in parishes. By about 1985 CLM groups were dwindling in parishes as new parish community appeared. The proportion of professionals in the Teams may have maintained their identity and adaptability to persevere in the changing world of the Church. Yet by the 2020s' Teams has also shown how the dwindling of young adult Catholics from 1970 has had an impact and numbers are not as great as in the past.

At the beginning of the 1990s the Adelaide Archdiocese launched an office for developing community in parishes. The office gradually developed a new movement called Community for the World. This later became Basic Ecclesial Communities, a challenging name. It later became Neighbourhood Church. This continued for ten years the Australian Cardijn model of personal action, but orientated to becoming the contact network of whole parishes. Instead of the hundreds involved in earlier movements, this for the first time regularly maintained friendship among thousands in parishes.

Student leaders in the 1980s

7

Student Years

ATF Press: After your early years with YCW you were involved as resident chaplain at Cabra College in Adelaide with a school YCS group, but then there was a period until the early 1970s where you had little contact with YCS. Can you start by telling us a bit about the earlier experience of involvement with YCS?

PR Wilkinson: In my time as chaplain at Cabra I was editor of *The Southern Cross*. I was involved with the school-based groups at Cabra and would have had little to do with the diocesan structure. The Cabra YCS in the 1960s was flourishing with many groups and very capable Dominican Sisters, teachers at the school, dedicated to the student.

Cabra may have had a dozen YCS class groups, one of the biggest YCS in Australia. I invited each class to nominate 'leaders' by their own lights. The same patterns of influence persevered year after year in each class. In this personal intervention I was faced with a choice, either doing nothing, or having no student organisation, as this preceded the rise of a genuine student movement with its own initiatives in the 1960s.

ATF Press: Then in the 1970s you were invited to be the national chaplain to the YCS by the bishops. How did that come about?

PR Wilkinson: There was much that was happening in the YCS and in society in the late 1960s. By 1972 the Church had experienced Vatican II with its focus on laity. Church attendance was at its peak. Youth were radicalising everywhere following advances in communication. There was a degree of sexual freedom following the development of contraception. Anti-war activism and the ending of colonialism had seen wide-spread radicalism for the first time since World War II.

My time with the secondary YCS was an introduction to a whole new world of Church, which radicalised me and challenged my nine years standard education in the seminary. I had been asked by the bishops to be the National Chaplain in 1972. I was thirty-nine years of age at the time, and I said I had been away from the national movements too long. I felt I was too old and that someone younger was needed. I declined and there was no chaplain that year.

The bishops invited me again the following year. I finally joined the national executive meeting in Melbourne in 1973. The team of four students I joined was made up of three long-haired boys and a girl, looking less radical but no less effective. My first novelty was being examined by the students as a job applicant. They interviewed me as to my social movement credentials. My links at the time with Aborigines of inner-city Adelaide possibly won me my spurs. That students should claim the right to accept me or not gave me heart. This was a student movement and from then on I saw it as my duty to believe in them and accompany them.

They may have looked unkempt by my black suited dress code at the time, but I was immediately impressed by their genuineness and fierce honesty. I began to discern over a year this thing they valued so much, authenticity. My training had been in orthodoxy with personal experience a scarcely examined value. My earlier orthodox experience had led me to treat any apparent conflict between traditional and personal experience as resolved simply from coming to a richer point of view. I was to become convinced that a Church authority might be profoundly wrong in its activities.

It was my conversion to a radical movement. Here was a very modest beginnings of a national movement like the International YCS which was becoming a stronger, in some places heroic, movement for change, particularly in struggles for democracy. In the Third World, student leaders were being killed by regimes. YCS was liable to be labelled by some in the Church as Marxist. Any prophetic movement for social justice runs that risk. Around the world other movements, radical movements in the Church, would be accused by some as being Marxist. It's worth noting that YCW in Australia was evolving similarly.

The complexity of that shift in everyone in youth movements is matter for a hundred academic studies and theses.

In this period, I alternated every month between being National YCS Chaplain in Melbourne and returning as the mild mannered *The Southern Cross* editor in Adelaide. I continued this for a year until Fr Pat Walsh MSC arrived to become full-time National Chaplain in 1974. He had dedicated his time to being close to grass roots YCS groups for years.

ATF Press: Going back slightly, please explain a little more about the 1970s in YCS.

PR Wilkinson: I was now identified as local YCS priest. In the late 1960s two Australian YCS leaders (Sue Carmen and Anthony Regan) attended a regional meeting in Singapore. In the 1970s an international YCS worker visited Australia and asked questions about Australian society. This was the first time that this had been asked of YCS in Australia by anyone. It was the beginning of a more sophisticated analysis of Australian society by the Australian YCS. At one analysis meeting we ran to a nearby bookshop to buy the *Australian Yearbook*, the sad sign of our total lack of Australian analysis.

This gave a new meaning to being a 'movement', in the same way as the women's movement was a 'movement'; a group moving in a common direction for change in society. When Kevin McDonald became International YCS Secretary in Paris during 1978 Australia was being recognised as part of a larger international movement.

Former secondary YCS Australian students initiated the Tertiary YCS in 1976. Internationally, YCS had long been predominantly a tertiary movement except in Asia and Australia. The new Tertiary YCS in Australia saw itself as a Catholic expression of the international student movement.

A new vision of YCS arrived from international encounters. The time of Mark Considine and Trevor Bate as Australian secondary YCS full-timers (early 1970s) was a time of questioning education systems with structural and social analysis. In the past there had been no trace of that anywhere in the Australian YCS. The number of Australian YCS groups was on the decline and by the time I moved into the national chaplaincy only eighty groups were left of what had been thousands. Nevertheless, YCS continued to be supported by the bishops with a full-time team with a life of its own.

The power of international anti-colonial, anti-capitalist university contacts left little time at the national level to recognise, respect and value the different path of Australian secondary students. The national leaders respected students personally. This was very basic. But student culture in the 1970s had little sympathy with the culture they had inherited.

In 1973 I was in Western Australia, on an official visitation of the YCS groups. I met with the student leaders and was discussing issues. It was a pretty tame affair with not much passion. So, I said to the meeting 'I do not sense much that you feel strongly about'. A girl who had been on the edge of the group and rather quiet said, yes, she had something to say. She told, in very un-convent language, a story of being forced to stand in the hot sun for an hour because no one had owned up to leaving their lunch order in the milk bottle, a serious contravention of the principal's orders. It was the first time I met an authentic criticism of the school system in YCS language not restrained by convent gentility.

In Ballarat, the year previously, a quiet YCS leader Mick Perkins (later on the National Team) had begun respectfully questioning the Brothers College ban on long hair. He argued that this would isolate the school from the rest of the town where long hair was the fashion, following the Beatles. There was a genuine and respectful debate ensued that term between students and school, with YCS students bringing out their own manifesto to oppose the ban. It would cost the leader his prefect's badge. This was an interesting and an unusual example.

In Hamilton, in 1971, a group of students even ran a cafe for young people. Already it was an example of a genuine student issue, an authentic student action.

In my brief chaplaincy the national YCS team declined its invitation to places of honour at the International Eucharistic Congress Mass in Melbourne. To their minds a long Congress contradicted the spirit of the Mass. I doubt they realised the mystified shock this sent through bishops who authorised their role.

One of the bishops I met at the time asked me, 'What is happening to the young people, Bob?' He was referring specifically to the YCS whose leaders were paid by the bishops. 'Keep faith in them' is all I could manage. Since 1944, almost twenty-five years, this docile student organisation had been a model of faithful Catholic youth. I now appreciate how removed the world of bishops can be from radical encounter.

The student leaders were more interested in authenticity than in preserving the nearly three decades of Catholic school YCS, a pride of Catholic education.

Neither bishops nor students enjoyed any history of conflict within the Australian Church. The bishops inclined to defend tradition when the students questioned it. YCS leaders on the contrary, were very aware of what was happening to their YCS colleagues in Vietnam, where the chaplains and leaders of YCS and YCW had been arrested and cramped into 'tiger cages', little better than animal pens for challenging the political regime. These young Australians were identifying with their opposite YCS numbers risking their lives under military dictatorship.

After my time, a few dedicated students would go on to question the school system but most young people began to feel the wind of recession. Radicalism lost its setting. In Adelaide, there were a number of fierce young radicals who were critical of the schools and the lack of student representation, but they were few in number and this did not last long in terms of others behind them. It did continue for a while with the national structure, but it moved back over time to trying to be more faithful to students in the schools, but I do not think it managed it. It seemed to run out of steam after my time.

New youth movements in the Catholic Church in Australia, like Antioch, were different in focus. Antioch was focused around an American priest, whose concept of youth work was much more addressing the emotional needs of students and people generally and was related to the Marriage Encounter movement. It was more centered around personal development and more explicitly a Catholic life, around the sacramental life, much more so than it was in the YCS or YCW. It was parish based and led many times by a married couple, who were the support group to the youth and were key persons in the groups. There was not necessarily a national or necessarily even a diocesan structure.

ATF Press: How was it you became Chaplain to Flinders University?

PR Wilkinson: I had been parish priest of Willunga, a small hills parish, for two years in the mid 1970s. Bishop Philip Kennedy asked me to transfer to being Chaplin to the University in 1976 (where I had been an part-time undergraduate student since 1967). I enjoyed the student years at Flinders. There was a regular weekly Mass for the student group on campus.

My time as the Chaplain at Flinders University coincided with the growth of the Tertiary YCS (TYCS), founded by former secondary school YCS leaders now at university. This group was accepted into the IYCS (international YCS) at a World Council of the YCS in 1978. Kevin McDonald, former Australian YCS full-timer, International Secretary of the YCS moved to Paris. With this, there was for the YCS in Australia a whole new opening to the international scene.

The TYCS was the first and only lay movement in Australia founded by lay people and was accepted by the Australian bishops as such. The secondary YCS was different as it had been founded in the 1940s by the Australian bishops. The TYCS gathered lay people searching for a fresh Catholic presence in society.

The book *Jesus Before Christianity,* by Albert Nolan OP (himself an ex YCS Chaplain in South Africa), became almost a textbook for the TYCS in Australia. It was a critical account of Jesus in the light of recent scholarship and the perspectives of Vatican II.

TYCS groups existed in Adelaide, Melbourne, Brisbane, Peth, with two full-time workers.

At that time, I was also chaplain to the decades-old TCFA (Tertiary Catholic Federation of Australia, previously UCFA). TCFA had been for many decades the national Catholic grouping within Australian universities. It long preceded the disciplined See-Judge-Act of society of the Intentional YCS. The leadership of TYCS and TCFA related well if not always easily.

At a personal level this was a period in which I participated in a number of international meetings, hearing students from developing countries describing their often life-threating struggles with tyranny. I remember one morning at breakfast in Spain, making conversation with a west African. I asked him of his experience of the student movement in his country. He mentioned calmly that he had been on death row for questioning his government. The international YCS started a campaign whereby the embassies and consulates of that country were flooded with match boxes carefully wrapped and sent by registered post. These required so much time and bother in getting signatures that ambassadors strongly recommended that the West African government get the troublesome student off their hands. Instead of being executed he was summarily expelled. I shared lamely that this was not a problem in Australia.

More profoundly I came to realise that an international movement for justice deals in life and death matters. It was a perspective that perseveres in me to this day. For Australians 'Social Justice' usually sounds like an optional extra. Outsiders might regard Australian internal affairs as the 'optional extra' secondary to life and death issues of international justice. Questions of climate change, for Australians can be seen as rarified, even fastidious. For children dying in a Third World dust bowl, clean air to breath and survive to adulthood is not fastidious.

There were students and priests at those International YCS meetings who were risking their lives on a daily basis under vicious regimes. These same students often moved into positions of national leadership once democracy opened up. Then a new question faced them, how a democratic leader reacts in the face of corruption. In newly democratic country after country the Catholic Church was poised between a safe blindness to corruption and violence or the huge risks of outspoken social awareness. Archbishop Romero of El Salvador shone out for challenging the tyrannical regime of his country. He was shot dead by security forces during Mass in one of his Churches. My own opposite number in South Vietnam, the YCS national chaplain, was imprisoned in the infamous tiger cages. I found myself powerfully aware of the risks I would want him to take for me, if he were free and I was in a tiger cage. A free country has the power and therefore the duty to challenge tyranny as a matter of urgency. In Australia we find it difficult to move from everyday reality to bother with questions of international justice.

The questions of international justice over a meal with the victims of prison and torture have a power to integrate the daily and the social that discussion groups back home found harder to achieve. The best of See-Judge-Act methods can limit itself to the everyday, without 'conscientisaton'. If a chaplain can share a passionate conviction that to be 'Catholic' is to think globally and act locally, he can extend the sense of action that is in the inquiry method to international issues. A priest/chaplain has the opportunity to experience and share 'conscientisation'. This was the term popularised by the women's movements for integration of the everyday within wider and deeper struggles. The hopes and fears, the joys and sorrows of every person are those of the Church said the Vatican Council. The chaplain's power to bring joys and sorrows, hopes and fears of the most distant societies to the fore as matters of urgency is waiting in the wings.

In my past while at school we gave our pennies to the mission box to buy 'black babies'. Today priests have the opportunity to show that the word 'catholic' is inseparable from seeing as brothers and sisters those in the most distant lands for whom the everyday is a struggle to exist and be free.

Standing outside the Empress Hotel in Sydney as YCS chaplain with Aborigines waiting for police to hassle them, served to integrate the daily and the political in a similar way to me.

This led me to a conviction that priesting must bring social justice perspectives into the 'normal' for Christians.

If there is to be a new vision of priesting it is all the more complex. Priests can and should be there supporting others in their lives, accompanying and encouraging people to discover their mission, to integrate their faith and life. But in today's complex Church and societal environment there is a real struggle to see how a new movement like the YCS or the YCW could develop. Possibly it is through a Catholic movement within the world environmental movement, as Cardijn saw within the worker movement. A Catholic presence in secular movements needs to be a partnership in the struggles and not as a secret society looking to control. Or it could possibly come from the national Catholic Youth gatherings with focused aims and objectives and follow-up meetings, similar to, but at the same time different from the YCW with its leaders' meetings.

Part of the genius of the Cardijn movements was their ability to integrate the daily and the political. This is especially the contribution of the Christian tradition to secular movements, to keep central the human and personal in every political issue.

ATF Press: Thank you for your thoughts on this era. In our next conversations, we will look at the transition to your work with the Basic Christian Communities in Adelaide, by looking first at your time in PNG.

John Momis.

8

'Yes, Minister'

ATF Press: Moving on to your time in Papua New Guinea, can you explain how that came about?

PR Wilkinson: This was by invitation from the Honourable Fr John Momis, who was a statesman and politician in the Papua New Guinea (PNG) parliament from Bougainville. He had been 'the father of the PNG constitution' and had been in politics for many years. He was a tribal leader in his home province in Buin, on Bougainville. He brought a fine intellect, along with his training for the priesthood, to share in one of the first independent governments of PNG. He was Minister for Decentralisation. (He was also to be one of the leaders of the Unilateral Declaration of Independence [UDI] for Bougainville. He was to become Papua New Guinea's Ambassador to China and later elected President of the region of Bougainville for two five-year terms.)

Momis formed the Centre for Concern (CFC), a committee of idealistic public servants and Church leaders concerned for social justice. In the 1980s he invited me to come to PNG to examine the prospects of a national youth movement for the nation. With leave approved by my diocese, I arrived in PNG as Private Secretary to the Minister for Decentralisation. I spent some months putting together a proposal for a national youth movement. My proposals were received by the committee, but this committee never decided on any priorities for action.

The Centre for Concern's idealism exceeded its skills in prioritising action. In PNG the tradition was to think of your family, your village, your clan. Only a few could envision this to be region or nation and this few had been co-opted by large multi-national companies. The

German Bishops overseas aid group had granted a million kina to the youth movement project. All were committed to their own admirable issues but unable to unite around one. In the end the funds had to be given back to the German Bishops untouched.

I was offered the role of director of the youth movement myself, but I thought one more expat analysing PNG was not needed. I declined the offer.

While working on the PNG project I was invited by Anthony Kelly to join his Masters degree course in community development at the University of Queensland, Brisbane.

PNG taught me a lot about community projects. But it also taught me that the experience of social movements in one country are not necessarily transferable to totally different settings.

I was inspired by the idealism of John Momis. His integrity was a light for his nation.

Fr Jose Marins

9

One For All

ATF Press: So, after PNG what did you do?

PR Wilkinson: I was invited to do a Masters degree in Social Administration at the University of Queensland for two years which lead to a research grant from the Australian Commonwealth Government. I undertook a Phd in sociology with a thesis on social movements in the Catholic Church. My thesis asked if there was a movement within the Church that was loyal but seeking radical change in its model

The hypothesis I tested was not of a cleavage between bishops and people, but rather a cleavage between bishop, priests and laity alike around a new model of Church. I concluded that there were only preliminary signs of such a movement. I interviewed groups of laity, literally by the dozen, who were not holding office in the Church. The participants were young and old, men and women, of various ethnic backgrounds (including an aboriginal poet) and of various educational levels. I found many people had questions about the current Church, but no alternative model became apparent. The subjects of the thesis referred to themselves as 'us', only in search of morning tea. Otherwise, their personal stories rarely led to the experiencing a shared project.

My three supervisors from three countries, asked for rewrites in different directions. History led me elsewhere.

At this time Sr Ruth Egar had been appointed as director of a substantial pastoral experiment in Adelaide. With her were two full-time workers and I was appointed chaplain. The project was nothing less than remodelling parishes at the service of better community life. A choice had to be made. I put the PhD rewrite to one side where it remains to this day. My time was now taken-up with the parishes experiment. We finally named this project Basic Ecclesial Communities, with a slightly provocative intent to distinguish it from several existing organisations with community ideals less focussed on this aspect.

The experiment started as a movement of Small Christian Communities (SCCs). Sister Ruth was the first to seek some way for an entire parish to be mobilised in renewal. Until that time parish renewal looked to *preaching* as the means. Sister Ruth was the first to recognise that the history of the lay apostolate had been the history usually of small groups of eight to twelve coming together for more intense formation and action. The excellent work of the Legion of Mary or the St Vincent de Paul Society was achieved by small groups reaching out to touch the lives of large numbers through a characteristic service of parish census-taking and practical welfare respectively. Yet this had always left the larger part of the parish not being mobilised in any lasting way.

Fr José Marins had been appointed by the Bishops of South America as their continental chaplain to the vigorous movement of Basic Christian Communities (BECs). He kindly accepted the invitation of the Catholic Archdiocese of Adelaide to visit us and introduced an invigorating perspective. The traditional parish had always been conceived as being similar to the solar system, with the priest at the centre. If five per cent of the parish were active around the priest, it would be regarded as a flourishing parish. Marins explained the BEC movement as a project to mobilise 100% of parishioners. Apparently, the method of doing this in South America was to establish four or five new model communities in different areas of the parish aiming to attract bigger numbers. Unaware of the Latin American limits, Adelaide Archdiocese aimed higher. The parish of Glenelg, for example, was mapped from the published results of the latest federal census. Details were available by Collectors Districts. It was possible to map neighbourhoods with some 200 Catholic homes in each. There were of course no personal details like names and addresses.

Many months of careful stages followed Marin's visit. The name of Small Christian Communities was replaced with Basic Ecclesial Communities. This name-change deliberately provoked a scrutiny by those interested in parish renewal and distinguished the project from previous community endeavours.

BECs would now first seek the cooperation of the Parish Pastoral Council and Parish priest. Then our BEC's team mapped a parish into small neighbourhoods of some 100 households. In the name of parish renewal, we painstakingly, one after another, invited a team of eight to introduce themselves to six or eight known parishioners in their mapped neighbourhood.

Each pastoral team listed from parish records the names and addresses in their neighbourhood. Each of the pastoral teams took twelve households near them. The parish priest sent a letter to every known Catholic parishioner announcing the hope of a richer community spirit in the parish. Each household would receive a visit from a nearby fellow parishioner with no other aim than being a friendlier parish. A key sentence of that letter read 'Be nice to them. It will be harder for them than for you'.

As chaplain the hardest step was personally inviting them each to visit their dozen households. This looked an overwhelming task until it was reduced to visiting one household each and coming back and sharing their results. Almost invariably the team members came back like the seventy-two in the gospel, rejoicing. To their amazement parishioners were invariably polite, usually friendly, and very often enthusiastic. Following the principle of gradualness, each team had accepted the contract of meeting weekly for six weeks. At each meeting they reflected on a gospel passage and went on to talk about their visits during the week.

Those encounters showed great promise of deeper pastoral analysis but the reality, while constantly enthusiastic, remained local. The pastoral teams did however achieve a 'neighbourhood parish'. Within a year there were 100 parishioners meeting fortnightly or monthly with real commitment to renewing the personal links now possible within their neighbourhood. Their speech changed from 'what is the parish doing' to 'what we are doing'. This pattern continued over ten years and the results were touching. An elderly parishioner had died suddenly. The priest met some relatives of the deceased who had come from interstate, apologising that he had not known the one who had died. They said 'Never mind, Father, the parish had been visiting him regularly'. The neighbourhood Pastoral Team had been visiting him as part of their task.

Every household in the parish had a friendly contact with another parishioner every quarter. A revolution had been achieved. That penetration of friendliness in vast metropolitan parishes had never been conceived of before. This meant not only Church-goers, but everybody listed previously for baptism, First Communion, schooling, marriage or funeral was welcomed as community.

It was an official work of the Archdiocese and was written up in the *Australasian Catholic Record*. BECs originated in the ideals of the renewal program led by David Shinnick in the 1980s.

ATF Press: What was different about BECs?

PR Wilkinson: What was different about BECs was prioritising the link between all parishioners. It succeeded in animating parishes to the point that experienced parish priests commended it. When Archbishop Philip Wilson arrived in 2000, he continued to fund the project. But by 2003, after eight years of BECs there were not enough fewer Mass goers to staff the intense BEC network. Benefits of BECs continued to be obvious for years in the 'Neighbourhood Church' concept.

Priests without previous experience of lay movements and the review of life, found the BEC model hard to appreciate. They saw community as admirable ideal but not really a priest's central responsibility. Some clergy could not see the daily life warranted a pastoral movement.

Do we lack the theory and the structures to relate our worship to what is happening to people? Nobody objects to the idea of honouring lay life, but there seems little passion to intensify, to deepen lives. Home, work and community considered in the light of the gospel had inspired YCW for decades. Ironically Vatican II focused on the inner life of the parish, an excellent focus, but again the rest of lay life became unintended collateral damage.

Why the Church is where it is today, with fewer people, is a very complex question. This is not solely a Church problem but one facing any group relying on the authority of the past. It is a societal problem, one which is facing many fine groups, like the Masons and Rotary, and all mainline Christian Churches.

Church attendance declined gradually from 1970. Steady increase in the Church attendance for twenty-five post-war years, from 1945 through to 1970, began to slow not peaking until the 1990s. Young people joined the Church in ever smaller numbers. The presumption today would be that parents who send their children to Catholic schools do not take part in the Church. They want their children to be introduced to Catholicism. The widely publicised Catholic clergy child abuse convictions have surely sped the slide from high esteem to the lowest.

ATF Press: Thanks Bob. The next interview will go a little further into your time with the BECs.

Fr Bob Egar and Bob Wilkinson travelling in Europe.
Bob Egar was parish priest in Glenelg, Adelaide.

10

'You Mean Everyone?'

ATF Press: Let us continue with the time of the Basic Christian Communities.

PR Wilkinson: We developed some beautiful achievements in BECs We followed a practice of testing our plans in parishes, aiming for a group of ten parishes with what had proved worthwhile, hoping results would speak for themselves beyond that.

In a little over a year in our first parish, in every neighbourhood parishioners were getting to know one another down the street as parishioners.

We started with a single mapped neighbourhood of seventy (two Collector Districts from the Federal Census), Catholic householdls in Glenelg. I had invited eight likely parishioners (OK, least unlikely parishioners) to a coffee in one of their homes. I named it as it was. We would try something small scale and see what we learnt,

For such an un-Australian act, it was a mixture of uncertainty and sheer loyalty to Father. I asked them to join a trial to drop by another parishioner near them just to say hello.

I promised if it was too hard or didn't work we would back off and abandon the plan. I promised six weekly meetings if they could, then we would evaluate. An informal letter had gone out the from the PP (parish priest) to all parishioners. It said the parish was trying to be friendly and nothing more. Somebody who lived down the street would drop by just to introduce themselves and say Hello.

Quite genuinely nothing further was in mind. The letter from the parish priest said, 'We are trying to be friendlier. If someone drops by be nice to them, as it's someone from down the street. Be nice to whoever drops by. It's not easy to do.'

I was a visitor too with them. We said a prayer and all said we would give it a go, expecting who knows what!

I found with the BEC's right through the 1990s there would have been thousands of encounters between neighbourhood leaders with people. In Glenelg there were eventually 100 leaders in a parish of about 4,000. They were quite unaware of speaking of the parish as 'them and us', rahter than 'we'

The explicitly religious occasion for meeting were quite varied. Lenten Ashes and All Souls days stood out in my mind. More common were picnics in the park.

ATF Press: Let us continue a little further with the time of the Basic Christian Communities.

PR Wilkinson: I am interested in developing a bit further the need for counter balancing the model of adult education with the experiential and the work that was achieved in Adelaide in the 1990s. When we started with the BEC's I was more or less given the whole Archdiocese to work with. We developed some pretty revolutionary stuff with trying the type of neighbourhood groups where people spoke about their experiences and their friendships and it worked very well and I eventually realised that the 'See, Judge, Act', is a bit of a facile formula and of itself does not work miracles. You can use it on a small scale for any project. But to build something significant that is really going to have an impact you need to look at the long term and that impact. But if you are thinking of some social impact, movements are not whistled up.

Kevin McDonald, who was a local leader of the YCS in Australia and then internationally, used to say, with a good deal of truth, that the YCS in Australia was not a movement. It approached it, but just did not have the energy that comes from a self-awareness of a movement.

I found with the BEC's right through the 1990s (there would have been thousands of encounters between neighbourhood leaders with people in groups, but it stayed at the level of personal encounters which never accumulated to sense of movement at all. There is always a complexity in moving beyond the personal to organisation or movement, of heading in a common direction, addressing common goals or interests collectively.

If you invite people to 'reflect on their life's', they often say 'thanks, but no thanks'. It worked much better when the Catholic Church had some moral authority and there were leaders who could instruct in the way of proceeding with a meeting, etc. The students were willing to accept the rules of the game as it were, including the inquiry mentality. But that does not exist now. People will not accept a method from the Church in the present era. So, while there is still some need for discovery, of people discovering their mission in daily life, to achieve that in the setting of faith is a difficult thing.

Alain Touraine, with whom I did my Phd research, had spent his whole life looking for a successor to the workers' movement, and looked at gay rights, women's and other movements. He found that only the women's movement had enough sense of change in the whole society. It lacked a model for society 'other than' the position of women in society.

This exercise here has left me a little humbled about just how much of a challenge globalizing a movement is. We are confronting a situation where the strings to the past have been cut and there is a milling about. I keep thinking of Jesus looking up at the multitude and he thought they were like sheep without a shepherd.

There is no longer the people in the Church to be organised in any way. Even if one found the perfect formula there is nobody there in great numbers to respond or implement it. In Cardijn's time it was very clear for the workers movement what the issues were and the way forward. People responded to it.

ATF Press: In the 1980s there was a document in the Adelaide Archdiocese entitled 'Community for the World'. Is it correct that you had some part in its drafting?

PR Wilkinson: I suggested some alterations in the original drafts, trying for a more clearly stated social analysis model, looking at the state of Australian society, and addressing the situation of the Church in this country. Put another way, I was hoping for a model based on the truth of reality, leading through to a truth of action, with a focus on small groups. What emerged was a focus on small groups, but one which had a limited understanding of the power that could happen through developing a wide based, broad understanding of the worth of small groups.

At the time of the document being written, Sr Ruth Egar was the full-time worker of the Neighourhood Church Program and was working in Glenelg. Her view was that we needed something for the whole parish. In the course of these discussions we met in Adelaide the continental organiser from Latin America of the Basic Christian

Communities (BEC's), Father José Marins. He gave us a powerful presentation of the 'solar system', where traditionally we had the priest in the centre and 5% of parishioners were involved and that it spread out with some at Church and others not going or involved. He said the aim of the Basic Christian Communities was to mobilise, animate or involve the 100%. I was jolted but determined to involve everyone in the Glenelg parish. If you live in the parish you belong to it. We remapped parishes into small neighbourhoods, so we had everyone included.

Father Marins returned later from South America a second time. His team were amazed that we'd attempted this and said that the best they'd been able to do in South America was set up a community in each neighbourhood and invite people to come.

ATF Press: Returning briefly to the experience of the YCW and YCS what points of comparison are there with the Neighbourhood Church?

PR Wilkinson: The radicalisation that occurred with the YCS and the YCW in the 1960s and 1970s did not touch our Neighbourhood Church in the 1990s. The CLM movement, that we have referred to already in these interviews slowly disappeared with women joining the work-force. CLM had depended largely, but not only on the network of women at home.

A form of globalisation is what radicalised the YCS and YCW around about 1970 whereby what was happening internationally began to have a bearing on the local movements here. Prior to that, both groups had been focused around the level of the personal, of taking personal responsibility for what was happening around them. The YCW in Australia had explicitly rejected Bob Santamaria's constant attempt for them to be the youth wing of his anti-communist movement into politics. The YCW in Australia had never hesitated in rejecting that view of themselves and of politics. The result was they avoided anything that might look like politics. When the YCW here did move, following the contact with the strong push against the Vietnam War, the international leaders suddenly came across people who had seen their fellow YCW leaders imprisoned or killed by the military. That really radicalised the leaders and the chaplains, which filtered through to the local movement in Australia. For the YCW as with YCS you suddenly had a radicalised leadership together. It always reminds me of the Polish situation in the post-soviet period, as there was a plaiting together of polish nationalism, the worker movement, and the religious movement of Catholicism. Those three together proved irresistible.

The beauty of books like Albert Nolan's *Jesus Before Christianity* was going back to a very simple theology, animated by the person of Jesus.

The faith of most Christians can be developed by courses, but unless it is inspired by the person of Jesus it is lacking. A certain passion is needed to translate faith into life that can be shared.

At the moment there is little conversation between people of faith and young people. The likes of the Hillsong Church etc, shows us something. Unless we can find some way of people coming together and having some kind of joy, some kind of religious experience and conversion for people, they won't be reached.

I feel I am back to the apprentice days again. How do we marry, what I think is crucial, the nature of formation with the needs of people of today?

This personal link of faith and life is none the less strengthened by organisation.

Evangelisation needs good organising, which is not everyone's cup of tea, as it is not everyone's vocation. It is a fact that many priests and people at parish level underestimate diocesan and national roles.

Dreaming and organising need one another.

It's the aim of this series of interviews.

ATF Press: Bob, thank you for taking us a bit further into this period of your involvement with the BEC's. Clearly, the method of work in the parish was similar to that of the YCW in your early years in Semaphore. Reaching out in small ways to meet people and show an interest. It was leaders once again showing a caring face and seeing where things could go. You, as chaplain, were accompanying leaders in their work, talking and listening to them.

In the next chapter, ATF Press will not ask any questions but leave it to you to summarise and conclude these interviews. The aim will be to bring together your many years of being a priest and to suggest, by returning to the title of these interviews, what new visions of priesting might look like.

Cover of the booklet prepared by Bob Wilkinson for the visit of
Monsignor Joseph Cardijn to Adelaide in 1958.

Monsignor Cardijn . . .

*The youth of South Australia welcome you with joy and
gratitude and thank God for the blessings which have come
to the world through you and the Y.C.W. which you founded.*

28th September, 1958.

11
Imagine

Matthew Beovich was named Archbishop of Adelaide in late 1939, when I was six years of age. He had formerly been the priest director of Catholic education in Melbourne and had authored a catechism which represented forward Catholic thinking for the day. For example, he taught the eternal salvation of those other than Catholics. This may seem simple good manners today, but not in the conflicted history of Ireland's popular Catholicism which Australia had inherited

Beovich showed a distinct vision for his diocese by establishing a minor seminary, at the invitation of the Holy See, in 1942. This was at the height of World War ll with its severe shortage of materials, a feat that must have taken some convincing of authorities in the most Protestant of the nation's six states. A minor seminary, probably now left behind as an institution, was a high school for students wanting to go on after school to study for priesthood at a major seminary. Within four years Beovich had established such a major seminary in Adelaide.

A steady enrolment of South Australian young men ensued. In 1950 the first student from this seminary was ordained, Len Faulkner, later to become archbishop of Adelaide.

I enrolled in the minor seminary in 1947 and was ordained a priest in 1955.

After four years as assistant priest in a parish, I joined the group of priests from the Adelaide seminary, all under thirty, who had been appointed to staff positions in the diocese such as director of education, inspector of schools, direct of social welfare social and chaplain of people's movements. I became editor of the Catholic weekly paper, *The Southern Cross.*

The former Irish officeholders had reached a seniority that warranted the honorary title of Monsignor, and they took up roles as parish priest.

This would all seem to have represented a pastoral goal of Beovich, one of the first Australian archbishops to strengthen an Australian culture throughout his diocese. He had experienced in Melbourne a strong Irish-Australian tradition, I think contentedly, but his direction in Adelaide was to strengthen an Australian identity.

A few months after I began with *The Southern Cross*, the Second Vatican Council was announced by Pope JohnXXlll. Such an event may happen once a century and this one was to shake the Church to it foundations. I was aged twenty-six and I was to have the role and the challenge of interpreting the Vatican Council to South Australia. I always felt totally supported in that by the archbishop, though I was too young to realise the understanding on his part that may have sometimes involved.

The young priests, I recall, were united in support of the Vatican Council. Not that we could have predicted its outcome. There was scarcely a voice of confusion or disagreement. The Council was seen to unfold in directions that encouraged us. In *The Southern Cross* I was inspired by publicising it. Throughout the '60s, we ran in the paper 'home discussion kits' for small groups to reflect on the Council's directions.

I was associated from ordination in the development of 'the apostolate of the laity', in Australia lay-led groups like YCW, the Young Christian Workers as outlined in first few chapters of this volume of interviews. At one time I was on the national committee of YCW. From 1963, I was president of the Catholic Press Association of Australia and New Zealand with Michael Costigan, editor of the Melbourne Catholic paper *The Advocate* as secretary, we tried to introduce a spirit of dialogue and encouraged public opinion in the Catholic press.

At an unofficial and previously unimaginable meeting of sixty Australian priests in 1969 at Coogee in Sydney, we shared a mood of energy for discussion, for dialogue, a sense of openness, an expectation that the priests would be heard. There was no doubt that there were those who would be named radical and those who were more conservative. But that meeting at Coogee I recall as being free from personal rancour. There were no cliques at the time. The Church seemed to be free of any organised groups that had taken positions. This was something that developed later in the Church. But at least until 1970 a general enthusiasm for the Vatican Council reigned throughout the world that I knew, certainly among the priests that I knew.

Among young priests as a diocesan paper editor, I was seen as middle-of-the-road in debates and as having some access to bishops. At the Coogee meeting I was elected as convenor of the committee to work towards a national association of priests such as other countries were acquiring. From this emerged, a year later, the first conference of the National Council of Priests which still flourishes with most priests as members and with a proud history of freely representing priests in Australia to the Church and to the world.

I remember correspondence with the bishops' conference but almost no enthusiasm in return. Priest's associations? What was the world coming to? I think the bishops were rather confused and uncertain about how to deal with a voluntary grouping of priests who seemed to be seeking a forum for their own discussion and presentation of viewpoints. Our committee was marked as young priests of energy and ideas but not necessarily proven in any pastoral field. Most were curates, parish assistants. We had untrammelled hopes of the Church at that time, including the hope of free association, and so it emerged.

For me, living in the world of the lay apostolate, the great tradition, the dominant Catholic energy in South Australia, in Australia before the Vatican Council was Catholic Action. This was a formal invitation initiative of Pope Pius XI in the 1920s to encourage and support lay people to return to public life after their long and shocked withdrawal following the Italian *Risorgimento,* the nationalist revolution that had suppressed the ancient papal states in the 1860s.

Catholic Action had been conceived as a project to assist the Italian bishops restore the Church to Italian public life. It was officially defined as 'the participation of the laity in the apostolate of the hierarchy'. Today this would be a very constrained view of the Church in society. At the time it was regarded as an honour for laity that the bishops should call for lay support in their role. That it would be a political role was self-evident in Italy.

But in Australia, after much study, the YCW became the leading vehicle of Catholic Action in Australia, very definitely removed from party politics of any kind. YCW was founded in Belgium by a young priest, Joseph Cardijn, 'to serve, educate and represent' young workers, to be led by and for the young. Its field was the home, work and leisure life of the young working class. This was a lay apostolate certainly inspired by the faith of the Church. But it addressed the experience of young workers far greater than Church. It was assumed its members were proud members of the Church, active as general members of their Church.

Unlike the Italian model, which was to represent the Church in politics, YCW focused on its belief in every person's God-given personal mission in daily life, home, work and leisure. It modelled in young workers hearts, the human and more-than-human possibilities latent in every circumstance of life, good or bad.

So, the Council was looked forward to. What we expected happened and we were confirmed in that; after a sharp struggle between the Vatican Curia and a majority of the bishops at the Council, a movement crystalised for the people as active, conscious and willing participants in the Church. That theme developed of the Church as more than a sacred organisation. In biblical terms, the Church was proclaimed as the *People of God*. This was not language we were accustomed to, but it was totally consistent with the thinking of our young priests of 1969. It was a theological language that well suited the particular dialogue of the Young Christian Workers.

We were priests supporting a young lay leadership in their twenties who were extremely confident and totally loyal to the Church. There was no awareness that conflict could ever arise between Church authority and lay initiative. It was not until the early seventies, the era of Vietnam, that conflict emerged over dissent. It was assumed up to and during the first steps of the priests' association that the solution was better organising to better implement the decisions of the Vatican Council.

Conflict among bishops over the Vietnam war had scarcely arisen; to begin there was little Catholic energy against the war, but it eventually developed. The Vatican had at this stage instructed the Australian bishops that the Church should neither *de jure* nor *de facto* be involved in politics or unions. The National Civic Council, the anti-communist movement of Santamaria maintained some sections of a Church-sponsored anti-communist organisation. My archdiocese in Adelaide, like Sydney, took a fairly clear stand, dissolving itself from its original anti-communist movement, and refusing its blessing for the subsequent National Civic Council.

I had a press debate with Bob Santamaria in the pages of the Melbourne *Advocate* after I advocated in an editorial the idea of a pause in the conduct of the Vietnam war. Val Noone, a Church historian, tells me that in this I was the first Australian Catholic voice to question Australia's involvement in Vietnam. I used a quotation from Pope Paul VI to suggest the pause.

The main division among the bishops would have been between the supporters of Santamaria, in his stance for the war against Vietnam's Communist rebels, and those who did not. Those who did not support Santamaria were generally bishops who supported YCW, which was strongly independent of Santamaria's anti-communist 'Movement', thanks to the united opposition of the priest-founder of the YCW in Australia, Frank Lombard, and Melbourne's long-lasting co-adjutor archbishop, Justin Symonds.

The outcome for most of us, unaware of this behind-the-scenes conflict, was that the YCW was non-partisan, with an independent commitment to lay people developing a sense of responsibility in their own lives.

The bishops apparently varied. Their point of union predominantly was obedience to Rome. They implemented the Second Vatican Council from a spirit of obedience. For Australian bishops and people then, once something was passed by Church authority, it was to be implemented. In Adelaide we had in short order a new-fangled senate of priests. Later we moved to a Diocesan Pastoral Council of the Laity, and we introduced English instead of Latin as our Liturgy language.

Programs were written to educate the people in the messages of the Vatican Council. The central theme was of the Church as community, to incorporate and transcend the traditional hierarchical model of Church.

The Southern Cross took the clear and consistent line of our Archbishop Beovich that it not become involved in politics and clearly not support the National Civic Council. I speak with some clarity because an uncle of mine was Bob Santamaria's lieutenant in South Australia. When I became editor in 1960, he approached me with some recorded tapes of Bob Santamaria's to introduce me to the National Civic Council.

Our Adelaide diocese funded an adult education-team, the Newman Institute with a vigorous lay leadership (originally members of Santamaria's movement). This ran a series of educational courses in theology, public speaking and social justice themes. I was named diocesan chaplain to help Brian Moylan develop this educational project. This mutated into the Christian Life Movement, almost an adult YCW, formed of many former YCW members as has been outlined in this volume.

Like YCW, the Christian Life Movement was based on a central belief that every person has a dignity and responsibility to be God's influencer in every situation life threw up.

It is hard to convey how strong that conviction was, that the laity had a distinct mission of equal dignity to the clergy. The mission of the priests was thus to help form laity in discovering and implementing their life choices as a sacred mission. The priests and people were to support each other's mission mutually.

Now the energies for the first priests' meeting in 1969 to form an association came from Perth, from Adelaide, from Melbourne, from Sydney, from Brisbane and from Hobart. Young Australian priests were inspired to share their mission. There was an energy for change. There were young and middle-aged priests at it, but I think it was an Australian Church, responding enthusiastically to the themes of the Vatican Council. This included a commitment and respect for the voice of the people and their right to question, to search for new questions and new ways. There were clearly other things than making headlines in the press, particularly the question of married clergy.

The question of birth control by artificial contraception was current in 1968 and the clergy were very challenged by where their duty lay in supporting the freedom of the people to make their own choice about this versus being the voice of the pope in *Humanae Vitae* against contraception. Some supported the laity in their freedom to choose to differ from the pope in such a delicate matter but would not have felt called to take a public position of dissent.

In the inner forum of conscience, there was already a good deal of movement in what people might choose. Young priests, and older, had had to make hesitant decisions of their role. The Vatican Council had already created a measure of freedom in questioning. This could and did lead many priests to question what had been long established, going beyond the Vatican Council. Catholics were seeking the Council's implementation in new forms that were yet unclear. Priests looked for an association not least in order to clarify questions in an ongoing dialogue rather than have any final set of propositions on a priest's duties.

For some priests YCW was a flagship of the future. Before the Vatican Council, it was almost the only carrier, implicitly, of renewal in the Church. And its theology was dominant; it was a very clear and explicit one that had been developed in the 1930s in Europe, for example in the French *Semains Sociales,* a series of annual events developing YCW style of studying social reality with matching critique and social program. YCW's see, judge, act method opened-up independent sources of energy. It was the experience of the people and of the priests with them that pursued the experience of the people.

This implicitly laid the course open for conflict in later years when that experience, and its implications, might not accord with an established line of the Church. It was not until the anticontraception papal letter *Humanae Vitae* in 1968 that dissent became universal within the Church. Many historians of the Vatican Council suggest that the Jocist movement, its methodology, its mindset in that independent listening to experience was one starting point of Vatican ll.

YCW did not begin its formation from a catechism course. It took people to their own lives. 'What's happened in the last week that you will do something about?' Certainly, YCW members also asked, 'What does the gospel say about this?'.

It used to be assumed that this would all be consistent with a Catholic belief. But over the half century since Vatican II, it is clear that experience is not altogether an energy superimposed on an official Church position. Young people today clearly start thinking from their experience and finish there. Any authority, including the Church, has to take its chances.

The period of the sixties marked an unrealised drifting apart within the Church alongside new ways of coming together. The priests founding the National Council of Priests were paying equal attention to experience and loyalty to authority. There was beginning a tension in that, and the drama of the priests' association was that unrecognised parting of the ways within the Church all in the name of renewal.

That a methodology and a mindset faithful to daily life experience was not necessarily going to stay easily yoked with official Church positions.

So, I simply went to that first seminal meeting of Australia's Catholic priests. I would have had some status of respectability among those priests by my position in the Catholic press. But priests of my vintage, or at least my circle, were preoccupied with the role of laity beyond the Church: clergy were not so prominent in my mind.

Some of us had so long been focussed on the meaning of life for the laity beyond Church that it took other priests who had grown up with Vatican ll to have their focus on internal Church affairs, on the need to modify Church structures for that.

I was thirty-five. I think those at the Coogee meeting may have been five years younger and closer to the Vatican Council's energies. My identity was probably earlier than the Vatican Council and while I assume that the YCW and the Council were coherent, I would have checked out the Vatican Council by its fidelity to my experience of YCW and its theology.

I would say, still, that the YCW surpassed the Council in its clarity and energy for a distinctly lay, human mission that was not at all the same as the role of the laity within the Church. Each was meant to serve the other but not to be confused. The Vatican Council directed its energies towards renewal of Church. There is a generation of priests, younger than I am, who were focused on the new Church that was coming and less identified with the role of the priest as supporter of the laity beyond Church. These were younger priests who wanted more clearly to shape a new clergy in its own right and not necessarily as single-mindedly at service of a lay movement. There is no element of conflict between these two roles but neither has there been a vital union of the two dimensions among priests or people. We lived the Council's public renewal of the Church, and we took our part in that very happily and with a shared sense of fulfilment.

There is a need to worry at this distinction like a terrier, always the case when anyone is tempted to agree too easily to a complex position. The field of reference of Cardijn—and I will take that as a shorthand for his larger insights that surpassed a youth movement such as the name YCW might convey—was larger than the Church. The Church was seen by those of vintage to be called to be at the service of the world, rather than the world being seen as a quarry to build the Church. Was that making less of Church? Not at all. But nor was it investigating the Church as fruitfully as Vatican ll had done. Blending tradition and new inspiration calls for a gift neither usually has in plenty.

My vintage was very confident, looking beyond Church towards lay life. The next generation of priests, and it rather puzzled me for a time, were more preoccupied with the development of parishes as communities and with new liturgy and maybe a new form of clergy.

The word 'ministry' of the laity came with the Vatican Council. The term 'ministry' connotes analogy to the role of the priest. The language from Cardijn before that was the 'mission' of the laity, which didn't have as strong overtones of Church. The words mission and ministry go well together for meaning, but their histories are different. 'Ministry of laity' connotes internal Church roles, whereas 'mission of the people' connotes a role in the whole of human affairs.

I was always a little uncomfortable with discussions of the ministry of the laity. While I agreed it was totally valid and vital. There was a role for the laity within the Church, which we had to learn, but the chosen role of my vintage was not primarily beyond Church . . . we took that somebody else was doing the 'ministry' work. There were experts about the renewal of the design of the Church and about lay language in the liturgy, this was the field of international experts and enthusiasts. I did not appreciate that my vintage, or the Cardijn slice of it, had a different agenda to the Vatican Council.

Ours was more clearly focused—and it stayed through the Council and afterwards—on trying to form a laity for their world. Whereas priests who came after me were much less focused on YCW, which was declining along with the decline of the workers' movement in the post-industrialised world.

If there was a fiercely strident post-industrial society, there was a post-industrial Church. Priests of my vintage were living with a declining movement of the laity. I'm repeating it too much, but young priests were focussed on the new Church in its own right. I've not seen that analysis written up very much. There was such focus on what the Vatican Council introduced that almost nobody has suggested that, in fact, it represented an unconscious risk of the Church being the whole site of renewal and attention.

To be provocative on my part, without intending to, the very attempt to provide a liturgy for the people and priests who welcomed lay councils, was Church restructuring. It was matched by a striking renewal of the religious orders of priests, brothers and nuns. These religious had special chapters, policy meetings; they reshaped themselves. Sisters, for example, modified the religious habits they wore. New structures developed which were different from structures of the past.

Those left out of that renewal, for lack of a structure, were the laity. The laity's ambition was to be heard within the Church. Whereas prior to that, for much better and much worse, the laity had to look beyond the Church to discover something in their own life.

Still, I would suggest that after the Vatican Council people *experienced* very little stimulation about their role in home life, work and society. The Church was and is caught in a circle of trying to renew itself internally without a matching sense of mission beyond. Just as it had tried to renew its mission beyond without a matching renewal within. It seems clear now that neither will flourish without the other.

My opinion is that fifty years of post-Vatican ll Catholicism has deprived lay life of a theology and a method to inspire a Christian perspective in sharing the mission of humanity. Where are young Catholics being inspired with a Christian sense of ecology and of social justice? Will history wonder that we could not see that internal and outward-looking Catholicism could only inspire one another?

My role through the seventies lay in developing an adult YCW in our own diocese, called the Christian Life Movement which was integrated in parishes by enthusiastic ex-YCWs especially. Subsequently in the eighties postgraduate study in religious sociology had little connection with the National Council of Priests. I have been a constant member of the NCP and pay an advance subscription. I was co-editor of its personal magazine. But Australia's Catholic formula has lacked something.

I am convinced that the Catholic Church in all its forms will only find its internal energy as it looks *also* beyond itself to questions of the world and about human beings. There is certainly a great humanity in the NCP journal, a sense of fraternity and solidarity among the priests, but dare I say less awareness of the big issues of society. It reads as it should as a club journal. Priests are very loyal, hard-working men who support each other. Their relationship and their questions like those of plumbers' unions and doctors' unions have to be mutual. But how to be more?

The key document of Vatican ll that might have made a difference was the magnificent manifesto *Church in the Modern World*, but that lacked a method. The method was potentially present in the Vatican Council document on the laity—it picked up the see, judge, act method but it lacked strong structures around the world.

What had been a spiritually energising thing for my generation of priests, from 1945 to 1965, for twenty years, was largely YCW. There was no adult version of that. There was the anti-communist movement, but that was rather separate and separated from YCW. A young lay person growing up in that era would have learned through their schools and their parishes that the laity had a role within the parish. There was very little energy for supporting the distinctly lay identity and lay life. Quite a drama and I think it is yet largely unattended to.

The postcolonial and post-industrial world was a time of deconstructing. It was a time of dissent and, on reflection, what could you point to that was a lay movement in society?

The social movements were movement for land rights, LGBT+, anti-apartheid measures, refugees and above all ecology of the planet. A Catholic's place in these often had no particular honour, not least because such a role as often as not involved dissent from some form of Church. Then the energy of the right wing from the seventies onwards in Western society brought new restoration mentalities among some priests and laity. I've not seen a lot of theological production or methodology for the many faces of the poor.

I became national chaplain of the Australia's new Tertiary YCS in the seventies which was rewarding work. These students' desire was to be authentic, faithful to their own experience and trying to understand where this was going. After eighteen years as a priest, it took me until a brief preliminary 1973 role with secondary school YCS as national chaplain to encounter even a mild radicalism of lay energies as described in these interviews.

Student opposition to the Vietnam War called on my support of them. Then I was to wince while I was national chaplain during an international Eucharistic Congress in Melbourne. The national team eighteen-year old's, were issued a thoughtful invitation to be present at the Congress youth Mass. They sent the invitation back to the bishops' committee declaring that Eucharist did not represent the Last Supper. Any structure that hinted or even might hint at a claim to some superiority was likely to be labelled structural oppression. The difficult thing was, of course, that real oppression is everywhere. Social justice is an apprenticeship in overcoming forms of oppression almost inextricably flourishing within the best of societies.

Priests' own model of fidelity to the Vatican Council and the Church was necessarily a struggle for justice in the face of gross or subtle oppression of all kinds. And that became a point of division when agreement with Church authority was at stake. Many priests and lay people felt that they could not stay faithful to the struggle of the workers, or of the poor, and stay within the Church organisation.

My argument in this series of interviews should not be contentious within the Church. It is for commitment to a full, conscious and active mutuality between fidelity to Christ within the Church and within the whole of humanity. What is more likely to be contentious is the understanding of fidelity beyond Church. In essentials unity, in non-essentials freedom, in all things charity (often attributed to St Augustine but also very confidently to early German Lutheran theologian Peter Meidelin).

New Visions

My vision of priesting is at the service of humanity. Earlier I saw the priest at the service of Catholics in their daily lives. I still see that, but now located within the mission of humanity to save the planet.

Has the goal of priesting changed for me? It has intensified not lessened. To be faithful to priesting is to be faithful to Jesus, 'God so loved the world'. The world for me is a richer vision than I started with.

The mission of the Church is the mission of the person in society. That mission has moved from improving the Church and humanity as a mutual project.

Liberation theologians like Gustavo Gutierrez and Albert Nolan OP, have said that they owe much to their experience in the Cardijn lay movements like the YCS and YCW. The see, judge, act method can be seen at the heart of their practice. Political struggle for the poor and oppressed, rarely highlight the formation of activists like these and yet it is clear in their writings that they do link the mission of the Church within the mission of humanity.

Integral formation

What elements are central to an integrated Christian formation? Formation is as varied as the people and the tasks. But certain elements are constant.

- First there is a *deep belief* in the mission of every person as the agent of God's love in their own circumstances.
- This mission only becomes real in people's experience by *observation* of their realities.
- If this belief and this observation are genuine their interaction creates an agenda ('action which is to be taken').

This program needs a growing understanding of ourselves as Christians and as human beings, never alone but together.

Concentric Settings

Society in Papua New Guinea (PNG) is built around the concept of *wantoks* (literally 'one talk'). Life is lived within the family, within the village, within the district, within the region. Since independence the task has been to discover the all-embracing single nation as *wantok*.

This concentric view of life is valid far beyond PNG. To be a Christian today is an invitation to constantly broaden our initial vision of our *wantoks*, family, religion and neighbourhood, to find broader solidarity across ethnicity, economic class, educational levels for starters.

Our sense of effective action requires an awareness of human solidarity. Solidarity is not naïve individualism, but creative tenson with shifting allies and opponents. There always will be both in the best of settings.

Technology and Ecology

Great social changes follow changes in technology. YCW after WW II flourished with the bicycle as transportation. The arrival of cars as common place was a major feature in the decline of parish life, especially in its youth forms like YCW. As young people more and more acquired vehicles, the parish shrank as one of their social locations.

The Church is inclined to continue its reliance on teaching and preaching for communication, but the inhabitants of this century look far more to electronic media. The current pandemic since 2020 has produced teams working from home. Already in parishes groups who meet face to face have successfully negotiated the shift to online meetings.

The Church has certainly invested in mass media, but older members are unaware that social media have become a new power in the land. Is there a parish that has committed itself to social media? More imaginatively, can a diocese build social media into a normal structure? Ethnic groups, shut-ins, study groups for example can not only succeed locally, but can leap all borders. Thousands of international encounters are springing up where previously a single laborious international event in a decade would have been the only meeting. Currently, the 2022 Australian Plenary Council has witnessed the influence of unofficial renewal groups united by on-line meetings. Post Council critiques have drawn large viewing audiences on-line.

New social movements will be more diverse at the grass roots than ever before as conversations between different language groups become normal. The single most powerful social movement is already the environmental movement. The actors in this are large rich nations vs poorer smaller nations. The Church's commitment to 'option for the poor' more and more will be an option for the poor nations. This is nothing new, but now emerges as the priority of social justice. Its main exponents tended to be experts but ease of international dialogue and communication between populations will give more and more weight to ordinary world citizens becoming normal.

The field of social justice is now global. The Church will find the meaning of 'catholic' as 'universal', presenting the Church as an outstanding model of global unity. Youth movements that look only to internal Church goals scarcely work anymore. The passion for young people is for global justice and unity. Where once a movement like YCW struggled for the working class, any new Church movement will struggle for the survival of humanity on our planet and especially for the survival of poorer nations.

The need for a spiritual influence in the environmental movement is profound. Posters like 'Climate Action Now', can be more or less humane in their goals. There are in fact profoundly human outcomes at stake in environmental debates. Climate can no longer be left to economists, any more than war can be left to generals. A century ago, Cardijn saw the class struggle as a religious question and shifted the tectonic plate of the Church. The scope of a simple movement was startling, and its effects were present in Vatican II.

The rate of growth of religious participation in climate action at a world level can and should be exponential. Are there leaders among the young who see that climate action is not an alternative to Church commitment but is demanded by fidelity to the gospel? The Gospel of John says that God 'so loved the world' that God's Son was sent to save it. Today God sends sons and daughters to save the planet and humanity.

For Cardijn, YCW was the Church in the working class and the working class in the Church. Today, the call is for a Christian environmental youth movement that is the Church in the ecology movement and the ecology movement in the Church.

New visions of priesting

So key elements of any fresh vision of priesting include:

- The priest is part of groups for whom world and Church are mutual, for whom person, Church and world are mutual. In itself, a grandmother talking about her grand-daughter's worries is as sacred as the parish council minutes. The search is forever how to relate them.
- The fidelity of the priest is to Christ, which is fidelity to the Church, which is fidelity to the world. This three-fold fidelity can be read in any order. Fidelity of any kind is a rare blessing, not be extinguished but to be enriched into fulness of fidelity.
- Individuals cannot transform the world. Persons can if they are linked as movements for social change. For the Church, more and more this means movements of lay people, by lay people, for lay people. The normal role of the priest in such movements is to animate, not direct.
- Catholic schools and Catholic universities have been the pride of the Church. Who can imagine a diocese without its education department? Formal education through lectures and courses is one thing. Informal formation through creative action and reflection is another. But each needs the other. Formation for action (structured movements of see, judge, act) is still almost a novelty. Priests have been more comfortable as formal educators, in teaching roles. Priests are invigorated within action/reflection groups.

- Where is the parish in this dream of mutuality? Clearly at present there is a widening chasm between the priests and the thousands who declare themselves Catholic in a federal census. The question is how to develop true relationships among people by the thousand. Neighbourhood Church with its own volunteer leadership, which means a smaller mapping within the present parish, is not only possible but surprisingly easy.
- It is possible to find a new corps of volunteers among those at Mass who will bring to life relationships of neighbourhood, with the priest as the animator and true believer in a new model of priesting. At the neighbourhood level, differences of race, class, education and so on can be bridged and become both a promise and a resource for an Australia 'where we are one, but we are many'.
- The sacraments are central. Sacraments always have been and always will be the action and the light of Christ. Fidelity to sacramental life means shining its light into the richness of human life. The Mass in particular awaits its discovery as the invitation to a new mutuality of God and people. The new covenant is a mutuality of God and people. Pope Francis has called for synodality. A neglected translation of this is 'mutuality'.

Movemented is a shared belief that the society we live in can be, should be and is being transformed. It is comparable to being in love in its power. It is not only a experience of transforming but being transformed together as a better world.

Whatever the twenty-first century brings, some lessons for me seem to be of lasting value.

Our faith as disciples of Christ is not meant to be a solitary or fragmented experience. The blessing of Christ is not a solitary affair. It is a consciously shared response to Jesus of the crowds. 'When he went ashore he saw a large crowd, and he had compassion on them, because they were like sheep without a shepherd. And he began to teach them many things' (Mk 6:34).

Recovery of the shared dimensions of Faith, Hope and Love.

I am convinced after my life with formation movements that there are three truths we are always called to keep in balance in the apostolate.

- Truth of Faith
- Truth of Reality
- Truth of Action.

Truth of Faith

The whole world now gives at least lip service to human rights. Many of these are rights to be treated well by others. But the greatest of our rights is to our mission on earth. We believe each person s created by a loving God. We are each a dream of love from all eternity with a unique destiny to shape with God our creation. Nor is this a separate destiny. The destiny of each of us is a shared fulfilment. Our destiny is to be loved, to know joy, beauty truth and goodness even by enduring suffering and limits.

That destiny does not begin at death but begins again every day as a mission to be the agent of God's love.

In what setting can such a mission be accomplished?

Where can it be?

When can it be?

The answer is always here and now. Our mission is in the actual circumstances, the good and the bad. Because that mission is to transform our real world into something better. The gifts of each and of all, always limited, have a purpose.

Truth of Reality

The truth of reality, or experience, is that there is much that gives life and meaning in our setting. But there is also much that deprives people of their worth. Reality includes ongoing injury from neglect or intent damaging body and soul. One of the neglected virtues is the wisdom to recognise what we are doing to each other.

There are actions that come and go, but the great harm and the great good is in the structures of life. As James Madison has said at the US Constitutional Convention in 1787: 'I believe that there ae more instances of the abridgement of the freedom of the people by gradual and silent encroachments of those in power, than by violent and sudden usurpations.'

Work places, homes and society can build in harms that are immeasurable. The world now recognises the harm that can be done to nature, to climate and to fertility. It would be a tragedy not to see the structures that are damaging and wasting humanity itself.

The creative tension from experiencing the contradiction between our destiny and our destructive situations can only be relieved by action to change situations, to make a difference. The action to transform the world always has personal elements, 'I did it my way'. But my way would not be true if it meant depriving others of their way. 'I did it my way' is often played at funerals. I wonder how often the singers believe that being my way and our way are always inseparable. My way and our way should be two facets of the same action. This is the truth of action.

Truth of Action

Truth of action is the path of being human, of being Christian. To some a shared life is hell, but Christ invites us with all great thinkers to see that life together is the only way to deepen human experience

The pastoral strategy of the Church is the sharing experience, faith and action and keeping them in balance.

Three words seem to summarise pastoral strategy for our time:

- Missionise
- Personalise
- Socialise

A Sunday morning Church can be an assembly of separate people. It is meant to be discovering together, envisaging together, acting together the modern world as being controlled by neo-liberalism, which means leaving the world to blind competition between individuals. It is incredible that the world should believe that blind action will result in human welfare.

Humanity is made to converse, to discover the common good in cooperation, self-limiting in oder to reach unlimited shared benefits.

Whereas the common threat today is destruction of the planet. The inner dimension of this is the destruction of the human heart and mind, our ultimate resource. The great struggle that provoked the modern industrial world was precisely the industrial revolution. This brought about an instrument that transformed 'the social question' of the workers into 'the social answer', the workers movement. This was a human creation that turned near absolute misery into the near heaven of modern conditions at their best. Through unity of voice and action over decades, the workers took their part in democratic countries to provide the unimaginable in education, health, social order and community structures for the common people.

YCW introduced the depthing of Industrial Liberation to reach the inner life of workers, not least in their faith and the Church. What movement could transcend YCW in its vigor and richness? To find this we need to re-examine the three Truths. What is the reality, what is the expression of faith, what is the extent of action?

In the Industrial Revolution of the nineteenth century it was a social class that was oppressed. It was factory workers deprived of truly human work. The poor of that society were the working class. Today the poor are not a social class. The poor of this century is humanity itself threatened in its very existence by a blind greed even to the scale of nuclear destruction. The route is marked by irreparable climate damage, sterilising of vegetation, the disappearance of water, the withering of beauty. The outrage is world-wide, not social class-wide.

The only answer is a true environmental movement to the scale of the problem. Voices and action to transform the climate of thinking. The contribution of the Church to the saving of the planet is to take its part in the environmental movement. The Church has always persevered in the formation of a collective mind to the dimensions of Christ. Traditionally this meant respect and care for the poor. But the saints of the twenty-first century include vast numbers committed to saving the planet without a belief in God or divine destiny. In earlier centuries, Christian missionaries headed for pagan nations. Today we are sent to one another and preaching is dialogue. Atheists may live and die in peace, but with the deepest respect Christians believe atheism is a deprivation even among the most heroic of hearts. Their heroism is in spite of their disbelief and not because of it. Let the dialogue begin. The world will not be finally beautiful, nor healthy, till it finds God.

By way of analogy there are those whose hurts have convinced them there is no such thing as love and truth, yet in spite of this they show heroic endurance and care. Their heroism contradicts their disbelief in humanity.

I would not presume to suggest a name for a global Christian movement for the planet (like Young Christian Environmentalist? It would not fit on a badge and too hard to spell). Some Christian global movement awaits its founders and leaders. There certainly are Christian organisations for the care of the environment, but whether there is a movement is arguable. Movements are not easily whistled-up.

In this series of interviews I have tried to give an account of one very limited priest's experience of movements. The priesting of the twenty-first century needs vision far beyond what has been offered here.

The central contributor to child sexual abuse in the Catholic Church ironically was what was to be known as the 'papal secret'. In the 1920s a secret decree by Pope Pius XI excommunicated bishops who involved police in cases of clergy misconduct. The decree was renewed over the decades, especially after communist regimes set out to systematically denigrate priests. I would argue that by thus looking at only one form of self-protection against scandal by total control, the papacy has caused a collateral damage that resulted in tens of thousands of children being denied protection. An essential element of the Catholic Church's reparation must be the commitment of its clergy to protect the children of the world by a movement that saves them from a planetary destruction.

In spite of this, clergy could be the occasion of a fresh collateral damage by talk of their ordination making them 'ontologically' superior, that is to say in their very existence superior. The idea of a permanent quality of soul from a sacrament was the defense of baptism by those who are not Catholics. The sad result was that this 'mark' of the soul was attributed to the ordination of priests as well. What was intending to convey the enduring effect of the sacrament, was then read as clergy, like the baptised, seeing themselves as superior to others. The example of Christ on the cross should convince those of this persuasion that the only ontological mark of Christians is their dedication to service.

Priesting in the twenty-first century is their dedication to accompanying all others in the common vocation to be more human.

Talk of ontological distinction of the priest is one fork, the other fork is to see priesting as an elder (presbyter/priest) as ontologically sharing the common human mission with Christ.

There is a *People of God* that is yet to come. My friend John Momis used to say: 'The last coconut tree has not been planted. The last copper has not been mined. The last baby has not been born.' The last Catholic Church has not come on stage. The last expression of humanity has not been reached. The ancients spoke of the 'obediential' capacity of humanity. Christians see that ultimate capacity for being human in Jesus Christ. There will be visions of priesting for a common humanity with God as Father of us all. The expressions of humanity are endless. Saint Paul was not speaking of uniformity, but endless creativity when he said to the fist Christians of Corinth 'When all things become Christ's, then the Son will become God's who made them so, so that God be all in all'.

To be Catholic means to be universal. To be open to all that is good and true, closed only to what is false and evil. Only a new heaven and a new earth will encompass that. A Church called to be at the heart of global rescue is called to be another world for freedom.

Bob Wilkinson as a young priest

CPSIA information can be obtained
at www.ICGtesting.com
Printed in the USA
JSHW081949100223
37570JS00002B/119

9 781922 737335